Collector's Guide
To
American Cartridge
Handguns

BY

DeWitt E. Sell, Ph.D.

THE STACKPOLE COMPANY
HARRISBURG, PENNSYLVANIA

Library of Congress Catalog Card Number: 63-9465

Printed and bound in the United States of America
by THE TELEGRAPH PRESS, established 1831,
Harrisburg, Pennsylvania

DEDICATED

*to my wife, RUBY JOANNE, for her
empathy and forbearance during
the preparation of this volume*

ACKNOWLEDGMENT

The author expresses his sincere appreciation to Drs. Everett A. Tracy and Duncan McConnell who provided a number of the obsolete handguns represented in photographic plates, figures one through thirteen.

Equal appreciation is due, and extended to, the following manufacturers who provided photos of their current line of handguns appearing in chapter eight: Colt's Patent Fire Arms Manufacturing Co., Inc.; Great Western Arms Co.; Harrington & Richardson, Inc.; The High Standard Manufacturing Corp.; Iver Johnson's Arms & Cycle Works, Inc.; Sturm, Ruger & Co., Inc.; Savage Arms Corp.; Sheridan Products, Inc.; Smith & Wesson, Inc.

D.E.S.

CONTENTS

LIST OF ILLUSTRATIONS

(Also see chapter 8—Current American Cartridge
Handguns)

CHAPTER 1

General Introduction

The American cartridge handgun has entered the second century of its history, having made its initial appearance in 1857 in the form of a seven-shot revolver of .22 rimfire caliber—the creation of the then new firm of Smith & Wesson. It is significant that the company which gave us this first American cartridge handgun is still playing a vital role in American industry and today produces the largest variety of handguns in the world. No other manufacturer has introduced more "firsts" in the evolution of the modern cartridge revolver.

Current cartridge handguns, be they revolvers or semi-automatics, appear to admit of little improvement. Whether today's product has attained its zenith remains to be seen but collectors are turning their attention to the antecedents of the modern cartridge handgun. These were produced in myriad variety and offer the collector a long-continuing challenge to acquire specimens representative of the many unique (sometimes freak) designs and mechanical devices.

Up until recently, the percussion pistol had captured the prime interest of handgun collectors—the early Colts and other cap-and-ball arms being the highly sought after and prized collectors items. While these types have not lost their fascination, they have become quite scarce and inordinately high-priced, thus compelling the collector of moderate means to turn his attention in other directions. With the cartridge handgun having passed its hundredth

1

birthday, those specimens of earlier vintage are now demanding increased attention among the gun collecting fraternity. These cartridge handguns of yesterday are sure to become the prized collectors items of tomorrow and the time to acquire what remains of the supply is today!

What information relative to American cartridge handguns is extant is widely scattered throughout books, magazines and catalogs. The objective of this book has been to bring together between two covers available information sufficient to furnish a guide through the labyrinth of cartridge handguns produced in America. Details with respect to obsolete models such as barrel shape, barrel lengths, finishes, grip material, etc. have been omitted for the most part unless they are particularly distinguishing of those models. Any unusual or distinguishing feature of a specific model is noted. The reader desiring more exhaustive treatment of some particular model is referred to the Bibliography of Suggested Readings.

As is true of any historical composition, the only originality that can be claimed is the recognition of the need for such a composition and the method employed in fulfilling that need. The author is himself a collector of American cartridge handguns and has been motivated to undertake this compendium out of his own felt need for a unified source of reference. The majority of gun collectors lean toward handguns and it is the author's hope that his effort will prove a time-saving and practical reference to both the neophyte and veteran collector as well as the general student of Americana.

The data cited in this book are as accurate as the references and documentary material consulted and only those sources which have been widely accepted as authentic were utilized. Supplementing this, the author has personally observed, and in many instances closely examined, the majority of handguns listed in this volume.

While there has existed at one time or another during the past century a plethora of individuals or concerns engaged in the manufacture of handguns (particularly revolvers), there have been only a relatively few who have survived for any length of time in the competitive struggle to arm American civilians. For this reason the major manufacturers of revolvers have been given more exhaustive treatment in a separate chapter from the minor manufacturers. Any categorization has a degree of arbitrariness but the criteria for "major" has been length of time in business and/or volume of units produced.

All companies appearing in chapter 2 (major manufacturers) are still in business with the exception of Hopkins & Allen. The only two major manufacturers to have begun operations in the twentieth century are High Standard and Ruger. Others have made the attempt but have failed to capture the public's fancy and in general were short-lived.

For the first twelve years following the introduction of its Number 1 cartridge revolver, Smith & Wesson enjoyed a virtual monopoly by reason of the exclusive rights it held for the use of Rollin White's patent of April 3, 1855, covering a cylinder with chambers bored through uniformly from front to rear—thus permitting cartridges to be loaded from the rear. This patent was extended to 1869 when further extension was denied, throwing the cartridge revolver field wide open to all entrepreneurs. There were several companies that infringed the patent right held by Smith & Wesson during the period it was in effect, this abuse eventuating in lawsuit verdicts in favor of Smith & Wesson. Thus there was a sizeable number of cartridge revolvers of various makes produced in addition to those of Smith & Wesson prior to 1869. If they were revolvers incorporating bored through cylinders loading from the rear, they were either infringements or, as in several instances, those licensed by Smith & Wesson who for a time were unable to meet production demands for these "new" revolvers using the self-contained powder, ball and primer cartridges.

Single and multiple-shot cartridge handguns, not incorporating a bored through cylinder, were being produced as early as 1858 since there was no patent preventing manufacture of cartridge handguns of this design. In addition, some manufacturers resorted to contriving cylinders which loaded from the front in order to circumvent the specific patent features restricted to Smith & Wesson.

The period from 1870 to about 1910 could be called the "Age of Pocket Pistols" in American firearms history. Those were the days when the pocket pistol was part and parcel of the fully-dressed "gentleman"—and ofttimes "lady" as well. There were pistols designated "bicycle" models—presumedly to afford protection to the rider while out in the countryside. This was the greatest period of variety and productivity in American handgun manufacture as is readily apparent by the numerous listings found in chapter 3.

As law enforcement became more rigid and widespread, and with the introduction of anti-gun legislation—particularly affecting the carrying of concealed weapons, the market for arming American civilians shrunk markedly.

For the purpose of more readily accessible reference, all American single shot pistols have been catalogued separately in chapter 4, all American multiple shot pistols in chapter 5 and all American semi-automatic pistols in chapter 6.

Chapter 7 discusses and evaluates the relative prospects of some ten sources for handgun collectors.

Chapter 8 catalogs, with pertinent specifications, all hand-guns currently being offered by American manufacturers as of their 1962 listings.

Chapter 9 features an extensive listing of most of the obsolete handguns cited in the body of the text with a dollar value assigned to each as of the 1962 gun collectors' market. These values are for handguns in "Excellent" condition as defined by the National Rifle Association covering both antique and modern firearms. The full rationale for the evaluation procedures employed by the author will be found as an introduction to chapter 9.

Abbreviations employed in the text are as defined below:

S.A. —Single Action	Derr.—Derringer
D.A. —Double Action	sp. tr.—spur trigger
T.B. —Top-Break	cyl. —cylinder
CF —Center-fire	bbl. —barrel
RF —Rimfire	Pat. —patented

CHAPTER 2

Revolvers: The Major Manufacturers

COLT

Samuel Colt was born at Hartford, Connecticut, July 19, 1814. He was granted his first United States patent on February 25, 1836. This patent was based on three principles: (1) the cocking of a hammer rotated a multi-chambered breech in a manner which aligned each chamber in succession with a single barrel; (2) the cocking action automatically locked the cylinder in position in preparation to fire; (3) each nipple, fitted with a percussion cap, was separated by a partition, thus insuring the discharge of only that chamber in line with the barrel.

On March 5, 1836, with the aid of financial backers, Samuel Colt set up the Patent Arms Manufacturing Company at Paterson, New Jersey. Here the first U. S.-made revolvers were turned out which are known to collectors as the "Colt Patersons." Later this plant also turned out revolving rifles, carbines and shotguns. The Patent Arms Mfg. Co. became insolvent and failed in 1843.

Five years later in 1848, Samuel Colt resumed operations in his own plant on Pearl Street, Hartford, Connecticut. Colt's Patent Fire Arms Manufacturing Company has been in continuous operation ever since. All firearms produced by Colt during his lifetime were of the percussion ignition system. He died at Hartford, Connecticut, on January 10, 1862.

Smith & Wesson's patent rights covering cartridge revolvers prevented Colt and others from producing this type until 1869. It was not until 1871, however, that Colt's brought out their first cartridge revolver. This was designated Colt's "Patent House Pistol." It was of .41 rimfire caliber with a four-chambered cylinder known to collectors as the "cloverleaf." It was the first Colt revolver of solid frame and the first Colt to incorporate an integral ejector rod. In 1873, Colt's introduced a whole series of cartridge revolvers which they termed their "New Line Pocket Revolvers."

Models of significance to the collector are detailed in chronological order. Asterisks indicate further reference in chapter 8.

Patent House Pistol (1871). .41 RF, 4-shot.
Distinguishing feature: "Cloverleaf" cylinder; recessed headspace for cartridges; fixed ejector rod.

Patent House Pistol (1871). .41 RF, 5-shot.
Distinguishing feature: Round cylinder; chambers not recessed for cartridge rims; no ejector rod.

Old Line or Open Top Pocket Revolver (1872). .22 Short or Long RF, 7-shot.
Distinguishing feature: Last design manufactured with detachable barrel.

Single Action Army* (1873). .45 Colt known as Army Model. .44-40 known as Frontier Six-Shooter. Also made in other calibers—all 6-shot.
Distinguishing feature: Solid frame; integral ejector rod in housing tube; contoured loading gate; plow handle grip.

Bisley Model (1896-1912). Same calibers as Single Action Army; 6-shot.
Distinguishing feature: Marked curve to grip. Target models had flat top-strap.

Storekeeper Model (1896-1912).
Distinguishing feature: Short barrel and no ejector rod.

New Line Pocket Revolvers (1873). .22 RF, .30 RF, .32 RF, .38 RF, .41 RF, and .41 CF.

Distinguishing feature: SA; circular sideplate; bird-head grips; spur trigger.

New Police Models (1873). .38 Short Colt; .38 Long Colt.

Distinguishing feature: Square butt; ejector rod; loading gate; police and thug figures embossed in hard rubber stocks.

New House Models (1873). .38 Long Colt; .41 Long Colt.

Distinguishing feature: Short barrels; no ejector rod; no figures on grips.

Double Action Revolver (1877-1910). .38 Long Colt was called "Lightning." .41 Long Colt was called "Thunderer."

Distinguishing feature: Last Colt and only double action Colt produced with bird-head grips.

Army & Fontier Revolver, Double Action (1878). .45 Colt; 6-shot.

Distinguishing feature: Military models incorporated lanyard ring in butt; normally 6-inch barrels.

Navy Revolver, Double Action (1889-1892). .38 Long Colt; .41 Short or Long Colt; 6-shot.

Distinguishing feature: First swing-out cylinder with split yoke frame model. Model sold to Navy was .38 cal., 6-inch barrel.

New Double Action Army & Navy Revolver (1892-1908). .38 Long Colt. There was no difference between the Army and Navy Models after 1902 with the exception of grips.

Alaskan Model, Double Action Revolver (1902). .44-40.

Distinguishing feature: Extra large trigger guard permitting firing with gloves, rounded grip with lanyard ring.

Figure 1. COLT REVOLVERS.
1. 1878 Army Double Action .45, 2. Officers Model Target .22. 3. Police Positive Target .22. 4. Single Action Army .45. 5. Army Special .38 Spl. 6. Open Top .22. 7. New Line .22.

Marine Corps Revolver, Double Action (1905-1908). .38 Long Colt.

Distinguishing feature: Narrow frame with grips slightly rounded at butt.

New Service Revolvers (1897-1943). .38-40, .44 Spl., .44-40, .45 Colt, .45 ACP, .455 Eley, .38 Spl., and .357 Magnum. New Service Target Model available in .44 Spl., .45 Colt, and .45 ACP.

Distinguishing feature: Largest frame of any Colt cartridge revolver.

Army & Navy Model (1909).

Marine Model (1909).

Model 1917 Army .45 ACP (1917).

Shooting Master Target Revolver (1932). .38 Spl., .357 Magnum, .44 Spl., .45 Colt, and .45 ACP.

Distinguishing feature: Tapered barrel; New Service (.45) frame.

Pocket Revolvers, Double Action (1895-1943). "New Pocket" .32 N.P.—discontinued in 1905; "Pocket Positive," .32 Police Positive, and .32 S&W Short or Long.

New Police Revolver (1896-1905). .32 Colt, .32 S&W, and .32 N.P.

Distinguishing feature: Longer grip than Pocket Positive.

Police Positive Revolver (1905-1943). .22 RF, .22 WRF, .32 Colt P.P., and .38 Colt P.P. Target models were made in .22 L.R. and .32 Colt P.P.

Police Positive Special Revolver*. (1907). .38 Special; .32-20.

Officers Model Revolvers* (1904). .38 Spl.; .22 L.R. (after 1930); .41 cal. frame target revolver.

Officers Model Target (1904).

Officers Model Special (1949).

Officers Model Match* (1953).

Army Special or Official Police (1908). Name changed to Official Police* in 1928. .32-20, .38 Spl., .41 Colt, and .22 L.R. (after 1930).

Detective Special Revolver* (1926).

Bankers' Special Revolver (1928-1945). .38 Colt P.P.; .22 L.R.

Distinguishing feature: Except for barrel length and special stocks, same in every respect as Police Positive.

Cobra* (1950).

Trooper* (1953).

Three-Fifty-Seven* (1953).

Python* (1955).

Agent* (1955).

Buntline Special* (1957).

Single Action Frontier Scout* (1958).

Buntline Scout* (1959).

HARRINGTON & RICHARDSON

In 1871 Franklin Wesson (a brother of Daniel B. and Edwin) formed a partnership with his 26 year old nephew, Gilbert Henderson Harrington, to develop a new shell-ejecting revolver which Harrington had invented.

Prior to the formation of this partnership, Franklin Wesson had been engaged in the manufacture of rifles and Gilbert Harrington had been employed by Ballard & Fairbanks. William Augustus Richardson, who had also been employed by Ballard & Fairbanks, was invited to join the new organization of Wesson & Harrington as plant manager. This arrangement persisted for three years when, in 1874, Gilbert Harrington bought out the interest of his partner and a new firm was formed under the name of Harrington & Richardson which has continued to the present day.

Harrington's "Shell-Ejector" model of 1871 was the first revolver with a cylinder that could be loaded and the

exploded shells removed by its integral sliding-ejector without removing the cylinder or detaching any component of the arm.

In 1876 the company brought out a second model revolver without integral ejector but with a spring catch for the cylinder. Harrington & Richardson had a handsome display case made for exhibiting twenty-four of their revolvers at the famous Centennial Exposition of 1876 held at Philadelphia. This historic, priceless, and artistic display case still exists in its original state and is housed at the factory in Worcester, Massachusetts.

The earliest models were all solid frame, spur trigger, single action revolvers. In 1878, H. & R. introduced the first of their numerous double action revolvers.

In 1894, the first of the buildings which comprise the present factory on Park Avenue, Worcester, Mass., was completed.

By 1907, more than 3,000,000 revolvers bearing the H. & R. trade-mark had been manufactured and distributed to the four corners of the earth. Neither Gilbert H. Harrington nor William A. Richardson lived to see their company reach its zenith of productivity or prosperity. Gilbert Harrington, though younger than Richardson, died first on June 22, 1897, at age fifty-two. Just prior to Thanksgiving that same year, Richardson died at age sixty-three.

The company had been incorporated in the year 1888 with Gilbert Harrington as president and William Richardson as treasurer. Following the death of the founders, Edwin C. Harrington, a son, was elected president, being but twenty years old at the time. Mrs. Mary A. Richardson

Figure 2. HARRINGTON & RICHARDSON REVOLVERS.
1. American Safety Hammer .32. 2. Sportsman Single Action, Model 199. 3. Model 922 Double Action. 4. Hunter Model Double Action. 5. Wesson & Harrington Model 1876 .38. 6. Wesson & Harrington "Shell Ejector" .22. 7. Model 45 Hammerless .32. 8. Premier Double Action .32.

became a member of the board of directors. A second younger son, John W. Harrington, joined the firm upon completing his education.

The first trade-mark of the firm was simply the letters H. & R. On May 14, 1889, a new trade-mark was registered—a target with five shots scored on it—and this appeared on the hard rubber stocks of most H. & R. revolvers until rubber stocks were discontinued. A final trade-mark that evolved is the still current H & R monogram incorporating the target symbol in its center.

Asterisks indicate further reference in chapter 8.

"Shell-Ejector" Model of 1871. .22 RF, .32 RF, and .38 RF. S.A.; sp. tr.; solid frame.

Distinguishing feature: Integral ejector attached to cylinder pin.

Model of 1876. .22 RF, .32 RF, and .38 RF. S.A.; sp. tr.; solid frame.

Distinguishing feature: Spring cylinder catch; no ejector.

Automatic Ejecting. Model 10: .32 S&W, 6-shot. Model 20: .38 S&W, 5-shot. D.A.; T.B.

Note: A special version of this model had a folding knife attached beneath the barrel which, when open, extended two inches beyond the four inch barrel.

Premier. Model 30: .22 RF, 7-shot. Model 35: .32 S&W, 5-shot. D.A.; T.B.

Bicycle. .22RF, 7-shot; .32 S&W, 5-shot.

Note: The Automatic Ejecting, Premier, and Bicycle revolvers were also made in special "Police" versions which were identical with the exception the hammer had no cocking spur.

Hammerless. Model 40: .22 RF, 7-shot. Model 45: .32 S&W, 5-shot, D.A.; T.B.

Hammerless: Model 50: .32 S&W, 6-shot. Model 55: .38 S&W, 5-shot.

Note: Models 50 and 55 were of heavier frame than Models 40 and 45. D.A.; T.B.

American. Model 60: .32 RF or .32 S&W, 6-shot. Model 65: .38 RF or .38 S&W, 5-shot. D.A.; solid frame.

Young America. Model 70: .22 RF, 7-shot. Model 73: .32 RF, 5-shot. Model 74: .32 S&W, 5-shot. D.A.; solid frame.

Vest Pocket. Model 77: .22 RF, 7-shot. Model 78: .32 S&W, 5-shot. D.A.; solid frame.

Distinguishing feature: Safety, or spurless hammer, 1⅛-inch barrel only.

Bulldog. .32 RF, 6-shot; .38 RF, 5-shot. D.A.; solid frame.

Distinguishing feature: 2½-inch barrel only.

Model 4. No. 80: .32 S&W, 6-shot. No. 83: .38 S&W, 5-shot. D.A.; solid frame.

Model 5. No. 90: .32 S&W, 5-shot. D.A.; solid frame.

Model 6. No. 96: .22 RF, 7-shot. D.A.; solid frame.

Note: The above three models were introduced in 1904, 1905, and 1906 respectively.

Sportsman*. Model 999: .22 RF, 9-shot; .22 WRF, 7-shot. D.A.; T.B.

Sportsman. Model 199: .22 RF, 9-shot. S.A.; T.B.

Ultra Sportsman. Model 777: .22 RF, 9-shot; short cyl. length of .22 L.R. S.A.; T.B.

Distinguished feature: Short action, or hammer-fall.

Eureka Sportsman. Model 196: .22 RF, 6-shot; short cyl. length of .22 L.R. S.A.; T.B.

Distinguishing feature: Short action, or hammer-fall.

New Defender. Model 299: .22 RF, 9-shot. D.A; T.B.

Note: Essentially a pocket version of Sportsman, Model 999.

Model 699. .22 RF, 6-shot. D.A.; T.B.

Distinguishing feature: Manual-operated ejector rod under barrel.

Target. Model 766: .22 RF, 7-shot. D.A.; T.B.

22 Special. Model 944: .22 RF, 9-shot; .22 WRF, 7-shot. D.A.; T.B.

Expert. Model 955: .22 RF, 9-shot; .22 WRF, 7-shot. D.A.; T.B.

Trapper. Model 722: .22 RF, 7-shot. D.A.; solid frame.

Hunter. Model 933: .22 RF, 9-shot. D.A.; solid frame.

Distinguishing feature: This was a 10-inch barrel version of Model 922.

Bobby. Model 15: .32 S&W, 6-shot. Model 25: .38 S&W, 5-shot. D.A.; T.B.

Note: These were made during World War II for London's police force.

Defender. .38 S&W, 5-shot. D.A.; T.B.

Note: This is essentially the "Bobby" model No. 25 rechristened for American civilian trade.

Model 922.

Model 622*.

Side-Kick—Model 929 & 930*.

Guardsman—Model 732 & 733*.

Ultra Side-Kick—Model 939*.

Gunfighter—Model 660.

Forty-Niner—Model 949*.

HIGH STANDARD

The High Standard Manufacturing Corporation is one of two (also Ruger) American handgun manufacturers entering business during this century to achieve success to a major degree. The firm had its origin in 1926 when Carl G. Swebilius, who had worked for the Marlin Firearms Company for a number of years, formed the company at New Haven to manufacture gun barrel drills.

In 1932, High Standard purchased the bankrupt Hartford Arms & Equipment Company of Hartford, Conn., and thereafter launched into the manufacture of a .22 caliber semi-automatic pistol which was designated the Model B and greatly resembled the pistols that Hartford had formerly produced. Several other models of .22 cal. semiautos were introduced prior to World War II (see chapter 6) but during the war years their expanded facilities were kept at peak capacity by military orders from England and the United States. Carl G. Swebilius died in 1948.

Civilian models of semi-automatics were resumed following World War II but it was not until 1955 that High Standard decided to enter the revolver field. It is remarkable, and quite a tribute to their designs, that their revolvers within the few years since then have acquired so significant a share of the market.

High Standard's initial revolver, designated the "Sentinel," was tagged by one writer for a firearms magazine as "the first new revolver in 50 years." In 1958, the "Sentinel Snub" with 2⅜" barrel became available in pink, turquoise and gold anodized aluminum frames as well as standard blue and nickel. In 1961, a deluxe version, the "Sentinel Imperial," was introduced.

High Standard's second notable entry (1958) in the revolver field was their uniquely designed "Double-Nine," a nine-shot double action swing-out cylinder model with the appearance of a Western style single action. In 1960 eight new variations of the basic "Double-Nine" model were introduced—six of these bearing the designation "Longhorn," the other two christened "Natchez" and "Posse."

High Standard has also produced both semi-automatics and revolvers for Sears, Roebuck & Company under the trade name of "J. C. Higgins."

High Standard (Hi-Standard) revolvers and year of

model introduction are listed. Further details are given in chapter 8.

Sentinel* (1955).

Note: The Sentinel is the first 9-shot .22 caliber revolver with swing-out cylinder ever manufactured. It was originally produced with choice of 6-inch or 3-inch barrel.

Sentinel Snub* (1958).

Sentinel Snub-Color* (1958).

Note: First revolver with colored anodized aluminum frame produced in United States.

Double-Nine* (1958).

Longhorn* (1960).

Posse* (1960).

Natchez* (1960).

Sentinel Imperial* (1961).

HOPKINS & ALLEN

The classification of the Hopkins & Allen Arms Company as a major manufacturer of American cartridge revolvers is hardly subject to challenge. Established in 1867 at Norwich, Connecticut, it was one of the few to remain in business into the twentieth century among the many firearms manufacturers which entered business following the Civil War. Hopkins & Allen were in continuous operation for some forty-eight years, finally terminating in 1915 when the property was sold to the Marlin-Rockwell Corporation.

Charles W. Hopkins and Samuel S. Hopkins were the principal founders of the company. Henry H. Hopkins, a third brother, contributed several patents to the firm but the extent of his involvement in the business is not historically clear. Charles H. Allen had been associated with Charles and Samuel Hopkins for some ten years prior to the company's founding and it is probable that he is the Allen represented in the firm's name.

Hopkins and Allen marketed their handguns through distributors up to 1898 after which time they dealt directly with the public. Prior to 1898, their products may, or may not, be marked with their name. They may bear just a distributor's name and a patent date, or be marked only with a model designation. After 1898, all H. & A. products bore the manufacturer's name. The marking "Hopkins & Allen Mfg. Co." was employed on their handguns despite the fact that advertising and catalogs bore the copy "Hopkins and Allen Arms Company."

The company was not incorporated until 1898. Samuel S. Hopkins retired from the business in 1901 and in 1902 the corporation absorbed the Forehand Arms Company. Charles W. Hopkins remained with the business until his death in 1914 and the following year it ceased operation as an independent corporation.

Inasmuch as many Hopkins & Allen products did not bear their name prior to 1898, the following patent dates of the company may prove useful in identifying various specimens:

March 28, 1871	January 27, 1885
April 27, 1875	January 5, 1886
June 29, 1875	August 21, 1906
May 27, 1879	

No models have been listed unless they have been positively established via: (1) the firm name; (2) the firm's patent dates or; (3) exclusive features covered by the firm's patents.

Blue Jacket No. 1. .22 RF Short, 7-shot; sp. tr.; solid frame.

Blue Jacket No. 1½. .22 RF Long, 7-shot; sp. tr.; solid frame.

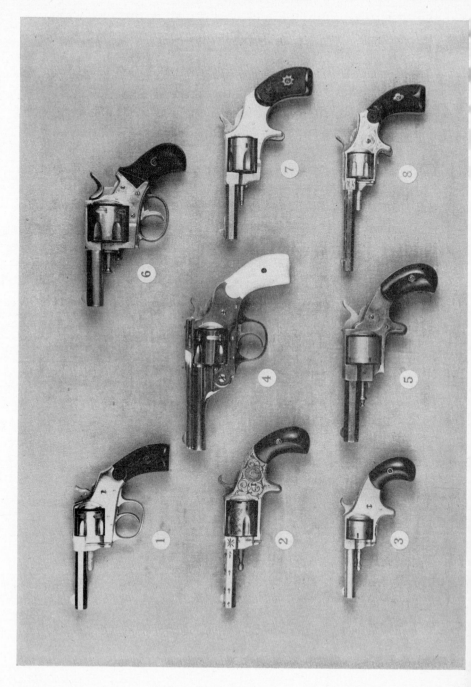

Blue Jacket No. 2. .32 RF; 5-shot; sp. tr.; solid frame. *Note:* The Blue Jacket series generally had rounded top-strap frames.

Allen-22. .22 RF, 7-shot; sp. tr.; solid frame; S.A.

Czar. .22 RF, 7-shot; sp. tr.; solid frame; S.A.

Capt. Jack. .22 RF, 7-shot; sp. tr.; solid frame; S.A.

Mountain Eagle. .32 RF, 5-shot; sp. tr.; solid frame; S.A.

Dictator or **Dictator No. 2.** .32 RF, 5-shot; sp. tr.; solid frame; S.A.

XL or XL No. 1. .22 RF, 7-shot; sp. tr.; solid frame; S.A.

XL No. 2. .30 RF, 5-shot; sp. tr.; solid frame; S.A.; safety cyl.

XL No. 3. .32 RF, 5-shot; sp. tr.; solid frame; S.A.; safety cyl.

XL No. 4. .38 RF, 5-shot; sp. tr.; solid frame; S.A. Also known as "Police Cartridge Revolver."

XL No. 5. .38 RF, 5-shot; sp. tr.; solid frame; S.A.; safety cyl. Highly engraved with log cabin scene on frame. Also produced in military and police style frame without safety cylinder in .38 S&W caliber.

XL No. 6 or **XL No. 7.** .41 RF, 5-shot; sp. tr.; solid frame; S.A.

Note: May have side-swing cylinder.

XLCR. .22 RF, 7-shot; sp. tr.; solid frame; S.A.

XL 30 Long. .30 RF, 5-shot; sp. tr.; solid frame; S.A.

Note: XL single action models generally had flat top-strap.

Ranger 22 Long or **No. 1.** .22 RF Long, 7-shot; sp. tr.; solid frame; S.A.

Figure 3. HOPKINS & ALLEN and FOREHAND &
WADSWORTH REVOLVERS.

1. H. & A. XL No. 3 Double Action .32. 2. H. & A. XL No. 3 Single Action .32.
3. H. & A. Blue Jacket No. 1 Single Action .22. 4. H. & A. Triple Action Safety
Police .38. 5. F. & W. Swamp Angel .41. 6. F. & W. British Bulldog. 38. 7. F. &
W. Russian Model .32. 8. H & A Czar. 22.

Ranger No. 2. .32 RF, 5-shot; sp. tr.; solid frame; S.A.

Scott. .38 RF, 5-shot; sp. tr.; solid frame; S.A.

Distinguishing feature: 24½-inch brass barrel, detachable stock available.

Tower's Police Safety Lock. .38 RF, 5-shot; sp. tr.; solid frame; S.A.

XL Police. .38 RF, 6-shot; solid frame; S.A.

XL Navy. .38 RF, 6-shot; solid frame; S.A.

Note: Sometimes classed as secondary martial revolver.

Model 1876 Army. .44-40 WCF, 6-shot; S.A.

Distinguishing feature: No top strap; hole in butt for lanyard.

Note: Sometimes classed as secondary martial revolver; made by H. & A. for the Merwin, Hulbert & Company. Also made in pocket version, D.A., with top strap.

With the advent of, and increasing demand for double action revolvers, an XL series was brought out in double action, solid frame models. Other later models were of top-break construction, both hammer and hammerless.

XL1 Double Action. .22 RF, solid frame; folding hammer spur.

XL 3 Double Action. .32 S&W, 5-shot, solid frame; folding hammer spur.

XL Double Action. .32 S&W, .38 S&W; solid frame; regular or folding hammer spur.

Distinguishing feature: Some models had the attached slide rod ejector.

XL Bulldog. .32 RF, .32 S&W, and .38 S&W; D.A.; solid frame; regular hammer or hinged-spur hammer.

Hammer "Automatic." .32 S&W, .38 S&W; D.A.; T.B.; regular or folding hammer spur.

Hammerless "Automatic." .32 S&W, .38 S&W; D.A.; T.B.; regular or folding hammer spur.

Range Model. .22 RF, .32 S&W, and .38 S&W; D.A.; solid frame.

Forehand Model. .32 S&W, .38 S&W; D.A.; T.B.

Safety Police. .22RF, .32 S&W, and .38 S&W; D.A.; T.B.

Distinguishing features: This revolver, patented August 21, 1906, had the ingenious triple-action safety feature. With the release of the trigger after firing, the hammer rises above the firing pin against a wall of steel. Also this model has a unique double-pincer barrel catch release.

IVER JOHNSON

Iver Johnson and Martin Bye formed a partnership in 1871, primarily to manufacture firearms. Both had been employees of Ethan Allen, a gunmaker who operated at Norwich, Conn., and, later, at Worcester, Mass. Their first shop consisted of two small rooms in the rear of a building located in Worcester, Mass. After moving to larger quarters in late 1872, Johnson & Bye commenced in early 1873 the manufacture of revolvers destined to make the name of Iver Johnson world-famous. This firm pioneered in the use of automatic machinery in firearms manufacture.

In 1883, Martin Bye sold his interest in the business to Iver Johnson. The firm of Johnson & Bye was dissolved and that of Iver Johnson's Arms & Cycle Works took its place. From the beginning, all Iver Johnson firearms had been marketed exclusively through the John P. Lovell Arms Co. of Boston. This policy remained in effect until 1895.

In 1891 the present location in Fitchburg, Massachusetts, was established. The fall of that year saw the new armory in full operation.

The Owl's Head trade-mark, used by Iver Johnson on his products and in his advertising, was also his mark as a

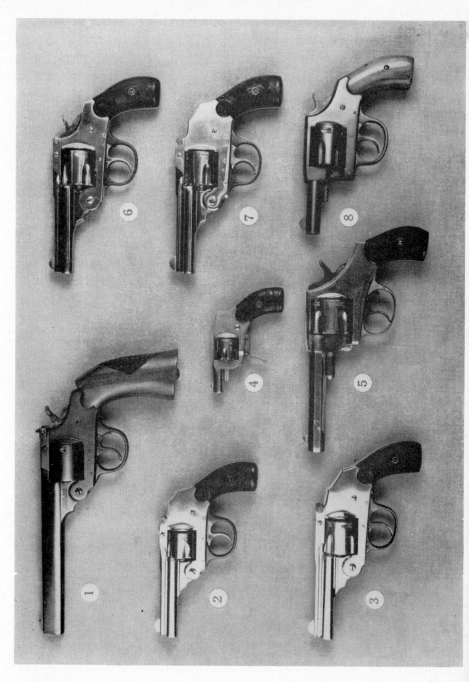

Chapter Mason. Iver Johnson died on August 3, 1895, leaving an industrial legacy to be carried on by his son, Fred I. Johnson.

During the first decade of the twentieth century, Iver Johnson was producing more revolvers than any other manufacturer in the world! Their "Hammer the Hammer" safety feature was so widely advertised that it became virtually a household slogan.

Favorite (1873-1884). .22 RF, .32 RF, .38 RF, and .44 Sh. RF; S. A.; sp. tr.; .22, 7-shot; others, 5-shot.

Tycoon (1873-1887). .22 RF, .32 RF, .38 RF, .44 Sh. RF; S.A.; sp. tr.; .22, 7-shot; others, 5-shot.

Encore (1874-1887). Similar to above models except barrel is round or semi-octagon instead of octagon.

Favorite Navy (1874-1887). Similar to Favorite except round or semi-octagon instead of octagon barrel.

Smoker (1875-1884). .38 S&W, S.A.; sp. tr.

Defender (1875-1895). .22 RF, .32 RF, and .38 RF; S.A.; sp. tr.; half-fluted cyl.; saw handle grip.

Eagle (1878-1886). .22 RF, .32 RF, .38 RF, .44 Sh. RF, and .38 S&W.

Distinguishing feature: First Iver Johnson double action revolver; solid frame.

British Bull Dog (1881-1882). D.A.; solid frame.

American Bull Dog (1882-1900). .22 RF, .32 RF, .38 RF, .32 S&W, .38 S&W, and .44 B.D. D.A.; nickel-plated finish only; solid frame.

Model 1879 Double Action (1883-1887). Cylinder swings to right on a pivoted arm below barrel for loading and ejecting.

Figure 4. IVER JOHNSON REVOLVERS.

1. Supershot, Model 844. 2. Safety Hammerless Automatic .32. 3. U. S. Revolver Co. Hammerless .38. 4. I. J. Petite .22. 5. American Bulldog .44. 6. Safety Hammer Automatic .38. 7. Safety Hammerless Automatic .38. 8. Sealed Eight, Model 68 S.

Boston Bull Dog (1887-1900). .22 RF, 32 S&W, and .38 S&W. D.A.; nickel finish only.

Swift (1890-1910). .38 S&W only. D. A.; hammer and hammerless models.

Distinguishing feature: Unique barrel catch of hammer model prevented frame from breaking with hammer down.

Safety Automatic Revolver (1892-1950). .32 S&W; .38 S&W; (1895) .22 RF. D.A.; hammer and (1894) hammerless models. This was the first Iver Johnson revolver to employ the "Hammer the Hammer" safety feature. In 1908 Safety Automatic revolvers were fitted with adjustable coil mainsprings and otherwise internally modified.

Model 1900. (1900-1947). .22 RF, 7-shot; .32 RF, .32 S&W, .38 S&W, 5-shot. D.A.; solid frame; loading gate.

U.S. Revolver Co. (1910-1930). .32 S&W; .38 S&W; .22 RF (hammer model only). D.A.; hammer and hammerless models.

Distinguishing feature: "U.S." molded in hard rubber grips—did not have "Hammer the Hammer" safety.

I. J. Petite. .22 RF Short baby hammerless revolver.

Distinguishing feature: Solid frame with 1-inch integral barrel; may well be the smallest revolver ever made in America.

Model 1900 Target (1925-1942). .22 RF (Short, Long, or Long Rifle); 7-shot.

Distinguishing feature: 6-inch or 9½-inch barrel; D.A.; checkered walnut grips.

.22 Supershot (1926-1931). .22 RF only, 7-shot; blue finish; 6-inch barrel.

Distinguishing feature: Marked in gold lettering on barrel "22 Supershot"—Safety hammer.

Model 69 Target (1929-1946). .22 RF only, 9-shot; 6-inch barrel; D.A.

Model 79 Target (1929-1946).
Distinguishing feature: Same as Model 69 except 10-inch barrel.

Model 90 .22 Supershot (1929-1949). D.A.; 9-shot, 6-inch barrel; cyl. not counterbored.

Model 833 Supershot Sealed Eight (1931-1955). .22 RF only, 8-shot; 6-inch barrel; D.A.; T.B.
Distinguishing feature: Marked on left side of barrel, "22 Supershot Sealed Eight"; counterbored chambers.

I. J. Target Sealed Eight (1931-1955). .22 RF only, 8-shot; D.A.; counterbored chambers. Model 68: 6-inch barrel; Model 68-S: 2½-inch barrel; Model 78: 10-inch barrel. (All models solid frame.)

I. J. Protector Model 84 (1933-1949). .22 RF; similar to Supershot Sealed Eight except 2½-inch barrel. Top-break; pocket style grips.

I. J. Champion Target Model 822 (1938-1948). .22 RF only; 8-shot; S.A.; T.B.
Distinguishing feature: Adjustable finger rest; polished hammer and trigger.

I. J. Trigger Cocking Target Model 36-T (1940-1947). .22 RF only, 8-shot; T.B.
Distinguishing feature: A unique action cocked the hammer on the first pull of the trigger and fired on second pull.

I. J. Supershot Model 844 (1955-1956). .22 RF only, 8-shot; D.A.; T.B.; adjustable sights.
Distinguishing feature: Last model produced with "Hammer the Hammer" safety feature; flash control cylinder.

I. J. Armsworth Model 855 (1955-1957). .22 RF only, 8-shot; S.A.; T.B.; adjustable sights.
Distinguishing feature: Adjustable finger rest; flash control cylinder.

Details concerning the following models appear in Chapter 8.

Model 55 Target (1955)
Model 55-S Cadet (1955)
Model 57 Target (1956)
Trailsman 66 (1958)
Trailsman 66 Snub (1959)
Sidewinder Model 50 (1961

REMINGTON

Eliphalet Remington made his first rifle at Ilion, New York, in 1816. His sons, Philo, Samuel, and Eliphalet, Jr. entered into partnership with their father in 1856 and the new firm of E. Remington & Sons was established. E. Remington, Sr. died at Ilion on August 12, 1861, and Philo assumed management of the partnership.

In 1865, E. Remington & Sons was incorporated. Samuel Remington died in 1882 at which time Philo bought his stock interest which made him the largest stockholder in the corporation. The corporation failed in 1886, going into receivership, but was reorganized in 1888 as the Remington Arms Company. Philo Remington died in 1889.

The first of Remington's cartridge handguns, the "Zig-Zag" revolving derringer patented by William H. Elliot, was introduced in 1861. This model proved impractical and less than a thousand were produced.

After the turn of the century, Remington concentrated almost exclusively on the development of shotguns and rifles. The famous Remington Double Derringer, with over-under barrels chambered for the .41 caliber rimfire cartridge, was maintained in production from 1866 to 1935 after which year the handgun field was abandoned by Remington. From 1918 to 1934, Remington produced their only model of semi-automatic pistol in .32 and .380 calibers.

Zig-Zag Derringer (1861-1862). .22 RF; D.A.; 6-shot; entire 6-bbl. cluster, or cyl., revolves. Patented by William H. Elliot August 17, 1858; May 29, 1860.

Distinguishing feature: Grooves on rear of barrel cluster, ring trigger.

Mason Patent Revolver. Pat. Nov. 25, 1865.

Distinguishing feature: Side-swing cylinder; simultaneous ejection.

New Line No. 1 (1873-1888). .30 RF; S.A.; 5-shot; solid frame.

Distinguishing feature: Unique integral ejector rod.

New Line No. 2 (1874-1888). .32 RF; S.A.; 5-shot; solid frame.

Distinguishing feature: Unique integral ejector rod.

New Line No. 3 (1875-1888). .38 RF; .38 S&W; 5-shot; solid frame; S.A.

Distinguishing feature: Unique integral ejector rod.

New Line No. 4 (1877-1888). .38 RF, .38 S&W, and .41 RF; 5-shot; solid frame; S.A.

Distinguishing feature: No ejector rod.

Note: The Remington New Line revolvers are also known as the "Remington-Smoot" revolvers. They were based on W. S. Smoot's patent of October 21, 1873.

Model 1875 Army (1875-1889). .44 Rem. CF, .44-40 and .45 Gov't; 6-shot; S.A.

Distinguishing feature: Web of metal under barrel; attached rod ejector; lanyard loop.

Iroquois (1878-1888). .22 RF; S.A.; 7-shot; solid frame.

Distinguishing feature: Small frame, no ejector.

Model 1890 Army (1890-1894). .44-40; 6-shot; S.A.

Distinguishing feature: No web of metal under barrel as in Model 1875.

Mexican Model (1891-1895). .38 S&W; D.A.; T.B.; 5-shot.

Distinguishing feature: This was the only standard type top-break made by Remington.

RUGER

The latest company to achieve wide acceptance by the American public, and one of only two (also High Standard) originating in this century to rate as a major manufacturer of handguns, Sturm, Ruger & Company was incorporated in 1949 by its founders, William Ruger and Alexander Sturm.

A small frame building in Southport, Connecticut, was the site of initial production. A standard, fixed-sight, semi-automatic .22 caliber pistol resembling the Luger shape, but with several unique design and construction features, was the first model offered by this firm.

By late 1951, the company was engaged in the development of a single action .22 caliber revolver that was destined to take its place as one of the truly outstanding American firearms. After Ruger announced their "Single-Six" revolver, they were deluged with orders—demand exceeding supply potential for an extensive period.

In 1955, Ruger expanded production to include a center-fire single action revolver chambered for the .357 Magnum cartridge which they gave the distinctive name "Blackhawk." This was followed by "Blackhawk" and "Super Blackhawk" models chambered for the most powerful factory-loaded revolver cartridge—the .44 Magnum.

To meet the sustained demand for its products, Sturm, Ruger & Company had a new compact, efficiency-designed factory constructed at Southport in 1958. Alexander Sturm died not long after the launching of this firm (1951) and William Ruger, an engineer, has guided the destiny of the enterprise almost from the first.

Ruger models and their year of introduction are shown below.

Single-Six (1952).

Note: This was the first single action .22 caliber revolver produced in America to be introduced in the twentieth century.

Blackhawk—.357 Magnum (1955).

Blackhawk—.44 Magnum (1956).

Bearcat (1958).

Single-Six Magnum—.22 WMR (1959).

Convertible Single-Six—.22 RF or .22 WMR (1961).

Super Blackhawk—.44 Magnum (1959).

Note: The only revolver made by Ruger which has been discontinued to date (1962) is the lightweight version of the Single-Six which was available with either aluminum or steel cylinder, had a frame of high tensile aluminum alloy and a 4⅝-inch steel barrel.

See chapter 8 for further details concerning Ruger models.

SMITH & WESSON

Daniel B. Wesson was born in 1825 and at age eighteen joined his elder brother Edwin who was already established as a gunmaker. Daniel remained with his brother until Edwin's death in 1850.

In 1851, Daniel joined the firm of Allen & Luther in Worcester, Massachusetts. Horace Smith also became an employee of Allen & Luther in 1851 and it was there that he and Daniel became acquainted and planned their eventual business relationship. Horace Smith had earned the title of "Master Gunmaker," having spent eighteen years at the Springfield Armory.

Horace Smith filed a patent for a "magazine firearm," patent rights being granted August 26, 1851. Smith & Wesson jointly filed a further patent with respect to a "magazine firearm" which was approved as of February 14, 1854. Shortly after this date, these two formed a partnership at Norwich, Connecticut, for the manufacture of a repeating pistol which became known as the "Volcanic." This particular venture of the partners was short-lived, as they sold their patent rights on these magazine firearms to a group who formed the Volcanic Repeating Arms Company in July, 1855.

Sometime in 1856, the firm of Smith & Wesson was reestablished at Springfield, Massachusetts, and began developmental work on their patented cartridge revolver which was introduced to the public in November, 1857— a seven-shot revolver firing a .22 caliber short rimfire cartridge which had been designed by the partners. From this point on the company has been in continuous operation. From the beginning it was a leader in developing uniformity and interchangeability of component parts in order to achieve volume production under quality control.

In 1874, Horace Smith sold his interest in the firm to his partner and retired. Daniel B. Wesson continued with the company until his death on August 4, 1906, at age eighty-one. Daniel's sons, Walter H. and Joseph H. Wesson, carried on the business. In 1909, the firm was incorporated with Walter H. Wesson as President. Joseph H. Wesson succeeded his brother as President in 1915. With the death of Joseph in 1920, the corporation's management passed to the third generation of Wessons.

Model No. 1. .22 RF (Short); 7-shot; sp. tr.; bottom-break with hinged top strap; S.A.

Distinguishing feature, First Issue: Round sideplate,

rounded frame with square butt, octagon barrel.

Note: Model No. 1, First Issue, was the first revolver made to use self-contained cartridges loading from the breech. It was designed as a "pocket" revolver.

Distinguishing feature, Second Issue: Irregular shaped sideplate, flat frame with square butt, octagon barrel.

Distinguishing feature, Third Issue: Irregular shaped sideplate, flat frame with rounded butt, bird-head grips, round ribbed barrel.

Model No. 2. .32 RF; 6-shot; sp. tr.; bottom-break with hinged top strap; S.A.

Distinguishing feature: Resembles Model No. 1, Second Issue; i.e., irregular shaped sideplate, flat frame with square butt, octagon barrel.

Note: This model with 6-inch barrel is referred to as the "Army" model, is a U.S. secondary martial revolver and was carried by some as a personal sidearm during the Civil War.

Model No. 1½. .32 RF; 5-shot; sp. tr.; bottom-break with hinged top strap.

Distinguishing feature, First Issue: Octagon barrel, square butt, cylinder stop in bottom strap beneath cylinder, single action.

Distinguishing feature, Second Issue: Resembles Model No. 1, Third Issue; i.e., irregular shaped sideplate, flat frame with rounded butt, bird-head grips, round ribbed barrel, single action.

New Model 32 or **New Model 1½.** .32 S&W; 5-shot; sp. tr.; T.B.; bird-head grips; S.A.

Note: This was the only single action revolver made by Smith and Wesson firing the .32 S&W cartridge.

Model No. 3 American. .44 S&W American, 6-shot; S.A.; T.B.

The First Issue was a U.S. martial revolver and as such

is known as "S & W Army Model, 1869."

Distinguishing feature: Long extractor housing under barrel.

The Second Issue had a minor modification of the barrel catch.

Note: This was Smith & Wesson's first revolver of top-break construction with simultaneous ejection from all cylinder chambers.

Model No. 3 Russian. .44 S&W Russian, 6-shot; S.A.; T.B.

Distinguishing feature: Saw handle grip; trigger guard has extension spur at rear for second finger; lanyard ring in butt; "knuckle" at top of back-strap.

Note: Over 200,000 of this model were produced for the Russian Imperial Army between 1870 and 1875.

Model No. 3 Turkish. .44 RF (Henry); 6-shot; S.A.; T.B.

Distinguishing feature: Similar to No. 3 American, First Issue, except modifications required for rimfire cartridges.

Model No. 3 Schofield. .45 S&W, 6-shot; S.A.; T.B.

Distinguishing feature: Unique barrel catch, hinged to frame, draws back for breaking open. This model's modifications were based on Schofield's patent of April 22, 1873. It was a U.S. martial revolver.

Note: A number of the Schofield model in 5-inch barrel length were sold to "Wells Fargo & Co., Express," and are so marked on the right side of the extractor housing.

New Model No. 3 American. .44 S&W Russian, 6-shot; S.A.; T.B.

Distinguishing feature: Short extractor housing under barrel; slightly rounded, flat bottom butt.

Note: This model, with necessary modifications for handling the .44-40 WCF cartridge of 1873, is known as "S&W Single Action Frontier."

New Model No. 2. .38 S&W, 5-shot; S.A.; T.B.; sp tr.

Distinguishing feature, First Issue: Long extractor housing under barrel, external cylinder stop at bottom-strap of frame, half-cock safety.

Note: This model has been dubbed the "Baby Russian" by collectors.

Distinguishing feature, Second Issue: Short extractor housing under barrel, internal cylinder stop, rebounding hammer.

Note (Third Issue): Similar to Second Issue with minor modifications. A variation of this issue is known as the "Single Action Mexican." Actually about 7,000 were sold to Russia rather than Mexico.

Model 32 Double Action. .32 S&W, 5-shot; D.A.; T.B.

Distinguishing feature, First Issue: Double series of stop notches on cylinder with free groove to accommodate action of rocker-type cylinder stop. Trigger guard straight at rear.

Distinguishing feature, Second Issue: Rocker-type cylinder stop and double series of stop notches on cylinder eliminated; spring-type cylinder stop incorporated.

Distinguishing feature, Third Issue: Symmetrical curved trigger guard.

Model 32 Safety Hammerless or **New Departure.** .32 S&W, 5-shot; D.A.; T.B.

Distinguishing feature, First Issue: Barrel catch released by pressing forward on thumb piece.

Distinguishing feature, Second Issue: T-shaped barrel catch released by raising hinged catch contoured to blend into tang of frame.

Model 38 Safety Hammerless or **New Departure.** .38 S&W, 5-shot; D.A.; T.B.

Distinguishing feature, First Issue: Z-bar barrel catch operated from left side of top-strap.

Distinguishing feature, Second Issue: Barrel catch hinged at rear of frame post, released by pressing down.

Distinguishing feature, Third Issue: Barrel catch hinged at rear of frame post, released by pressing forward on thumb piece.

Distinguishing feature, Fourth Issue: T-shaped barrel catch released by raising hinged catch contoured to blend into tang of frame.

Distinguishing feature, Fifth Issue: Same as Fourth Issue except the front sight is a solidly forged part of barrel.

Note: The "Safety Hammerless" models have a safety lever incorporated into the back-strap which must be squeezed in to permit operation of the trigger. These models have been dubbed "Lemon Squeezers" by collectors. They were discontinued about 1941.

Model 38 Double Action. .38 S&W, 5-shot; D.A.; T.B.

Distinguishing feature, First Issue: Square sideplate; double series of stop notches on cylinder with free groove to accommodate rocker-type cylinder stop.

Distinguishing feature, Second Issue: Irregular sideplate; rocker-type cylinder stop with double stop notches on cylinder eliminated.

Distinguishing feature, Third Issue: Internal modifications only; First, Second, and Third Issues have the straight-back trigger guard.

Distinguishing feature, Fourth Issue: Shape of trigger guard altered; pinned front sight.

Distinguishing feature, Fifth Issue: Same as Fourth Issue except front sight is a solidly forged part of the barrel.

Note: Over 500,000 of this model were produced throughout its run of issues. Discontinued 1911.

Model 38 Perfected Double Action. .38 S&W; 5-shot; D.A.; T.B.

Figure 5. SMITH & WESSON REVOLVERS.

1. Perfected Double Action .38. 2. Model "M" Hand Ejector, 2nd Issue .22. 3. Model "I" Hand Ejector, 1st Issue .32. 4. Military & Police, Round Butt .38 Spl. 5. Model No. 2 "Army." 6. Safety Hammerless, 1st Issue .32. 7. Safety Hammerless, 2nd Issue. 32. 8. Model No. 1, 3rd Issue .22.

Distinguishing feature: Readily identifiable by release latch on left side of frame which must be pushed forward before barrel can be broken open at the top; it is the only model with this double-release feature.

Model I Hand Ejector. .32 S&W Long; 6-shot, D.A.; swing-out cyl.

Distinguishing feature: Cylinder stop on top-strap; no forward extractor rod locking lug under barrel; no release catch on the left side of the frame.

Note: This was the first S&W model with a split-yoke frame and swing-out cylinder. This model has been modified numerous times over the years and is still being manufactured as the "Hand Ejector, Model 30."

Regulation Police Model 32. .32 S&W Long, 6-shot; D.A.; swing-out cyl.

Note: This model started with Serial No. 331,320 and incorporated a forward locking lug under the barrel for the extractor rod.

Regulation Police Model 38. .38 S&W, 5-shot; D.A.; swing-out cyl.

Distinguishing feature: Made in 4-inch barrel length only; started with serial number 1 in 1917.

Military and Police Model. .38 Long Colt, 6-shot; D.A.; swing-out cyl.

Distinguishing feature, First Issue: No forward locking lug under the barrel for the extractor rod; cylinder release latch on the left side of the frame. It is sometimes referred to as Model 1899 ARMY-NAVY; 2,000 were ordered by the U.S. Navy, 1,000 were ordered by the U.S. Army. Military models had a lanyard ring in the butt.

Note: The Military and Police model has gone through numerous modifications over the years and continues to be among S&W's top-sellers. Since the advent of the .38 S&W Special (about 1900), it has been chambered primarily for this cartridge. Since the Military & Police Model, Issue of 1902, the forward locking lug under the barrel has been incorporated for an extractor rod.

Model 44 Double Action. .44 S&W Russian, 6-shot; D.A.; T.B.

Distinguishing feature: Straight-back trigger guard; discontinued 1913.

Model 44 Double Action Frontier. .44-40 WCF, 6-shot; D.A.; T.B.

Model New Century. .44 S&W Spl.; 6-shot; D.A.; swing-out cyl.

Distinguishing feature: Has a housing under the barrel for the extractor rod and an extractor rod locking lug. It was the first model to incorporate this type housing.

Note: The New Century is known to collectors as the "Triple Lock."

Model 32-20 Hand Ejector. .32-20 WCF, 6-shot; D.A.; swing-out cyl.

Note: Similar to the Military & Police model, it was constructed along similar lines and evolved through the same stages of development.

Model of 1891. .38 S&W, 5-shot; S.A.; T.B.

Note: From 1893 to 1895, this model's frame could be used with interchangeable single shot barrels in calibers .38 S&W, .32 S&W, and .22 Long Rifle. It could be fitted with target stocks.

Model M Hand Ejector. .22 RF, 7-shot; D.A.; swing-out cyl.

Distinguishing feature, First Issue: Knurled button-shaped cylinder release on left side of frame; no extractor rod locking lug under barrel.

Distinguishing feature, Second Issue: No cylinder release latch on frame; locking lug for extractor rod is under the barrel with a spring-actuated release knob.

Distinguishing feature, Third Issue: No cylinder release

latch on the frame; rebounding hammer; only issue available with barrel longer than 3½ inches (up to 6 inches). This issue was catalogued as the "22 Perfected Hand Ejector."

Note: These three issues of the Model M Hand Ejector have long been called "Ladysmiths" due to their small size and appeal to women. They are in great demand among collectors, which has forced their value to an inordinate height out of keeping with either their utility or vintage. There were 26,154 of Model M-H.E. manufactured.

Model 22/32 Hand Ejector. .22 RF, 6-shot; D.A.; swing-out cyl. Catalogued as "22/32 Heavy Frame Target Revolver."

Distinguishing feature: Frame similar to 32 Hand Ejector, Issue of 1903; 6-inch barrel only, target sights and stock.

Note: Collectors know this as the "Bekeart Model."

Model 1917 Army. .45 ACP or .45 AR; 6-shot; D.A.; swing-out cyl.

Distinguishing feature: Lanyard ring in butt; blue only; 5½-inch barrel.

Note: There were 175,000 furnished the U.S. Government during World War I. The model was available to the civilian trade up to World War II.

Victory Model. .38 S&W Spl.; .38 S&W; 6-shot; D.A.; swing-out cyl.

Distinguishing feature: Military & Police frame; Parkerized finish, plain wood stocks, lanyard ring in butt.

Note: World War II military model was made for U.S. and British Governments.

For data regarding the following Smith and Wesson Models, which are more recent, see chapter 8.

357 Magnum
44 Magnum
38/44 Heavy Duty
1950 44 Military
Highway Patrolman
38/44 Outdoorsman
1950 44 Target
1950 45 Target
1955 45 Target
1950 Army
357 Combat Magnum
38 Military and Police
38 Military and Police
  Airweight
K-22 Masterpiece

K-32 Masterpiece
K-38 Masterpiece
Combat Masterpiece
1953 22/32 Target
1953 22/32 Kit Gun
1955 22/32 Kit Gun
  Airweight
38 Terrier
32 Hand Ejector
38 Chiefs Special
Chiefs Special Airweight
Bodyguard
Centennial
32 Regulation Police
38 Regulation Police
22 Magnum Center Fire

CHAPTER 3

Revolvers: The Minor Manufacturers

With the termination of Rollin White's patent in 1869, it was not long before the market was being flooded with cartridge revolvers—the majority of which were cheaply constructed to appeal to the economy-minded and to be competitive with the single shot pistols of the day. Single-action, solid frame, spur trigger cartridge revolvers, generally nickel-plated, dominated the first twenty years of the "Age of Pocket Pistols." They were displaced to a considerable extent with the advent of double-action revolvers.

Mail order houses of the period blazoned the unique virtues of their particular brand names although identical handguns by the same maker (unmarked) were being offered by other competitors under differing brand names.

Post office regulations finally brought this era of handguns via parcel post to a close and handguns were henceforth distributed by manufacturers under their own name via bona fide licensed dealers in firearms.

AETNA ARMS CO. (1880-1890) New York, N. Y.
.22 RF. 7-shot; S.A.; sp. tr.; solid frame.
.32 RF. 5-shot; S.A.; sp. tr.; solid frame.

ALLEN, ETHAN & CO. (1865-1871) Worcester, Mass.
.22 RF. 7-shot; S.A.; sp. tr.; solid frame, side hammer.
.32 RF. 6-shot; S.A.; sp. tr.; solid frame, side hammer.

ALLEN & WHEELOCK (1856-1865) Worcester, Mass.
Manufactured single action solid frame revolvers with side hammers in calibers .22, .32, .38, and .44. In some

models the cylinder pin is inserted from the rear. These were infringements of the Rollin White patent held by Smith & Wesson. Also manufactured the Allen lip cartridge revolvers in calibers .25, .32, .38, and .44.

AMERICAN ARMS COMPANY (1861-1904) Boston, Mass.
.38 S&W. 5-shot; S.A.; sp. tr.; T.B.

Distinguishing feature: Manually-operated extractor ring at the rear of cylinder of slightly greater circumference than cylinder; also double flutes between each chamber of cylinder. This company also manufactured both single action and double action revolvers in calibers .32, .38, and .41.

AMERICAN STANDARD TOOL CO. (1860-1881) Newark, N. J.
.22 RF. 7-shot; S.A.; sp. tr.; bottom-break as in Smith & Wesson's No. 1.

BACON MANUFACTURING CO. (1852-1891) Norwich, Conn.

Manufactured the following "Name Brand" .22 RF, 7-shot, S.A. solid frame revolvers: Bonanza, Conqueror, Daisy, Express, Guardian, Little Giant. The Conqueror was also produced in .32 RF, .38 RF, and .41 RF. All the above were produced under the patent of A. L. Sweet, December 10, 1878. The firm also manufactured cartridge revolvers under the patent of C. W. Hopkins dated May 27, 1862.
.38 RF. 6-shot; S.A.; solid frame; sp. tr.; "Navy."

Distinguishing feature: With a 7½-inch barrel, this model is considered by collectors an American secondary martial revolver.

BALLARD & FAIRBANKS (1870-1872) Worcester, Mass., BALLARD & CO., C. H., (1861-1869). No reliable information available on this firm's cartridge revolvers.

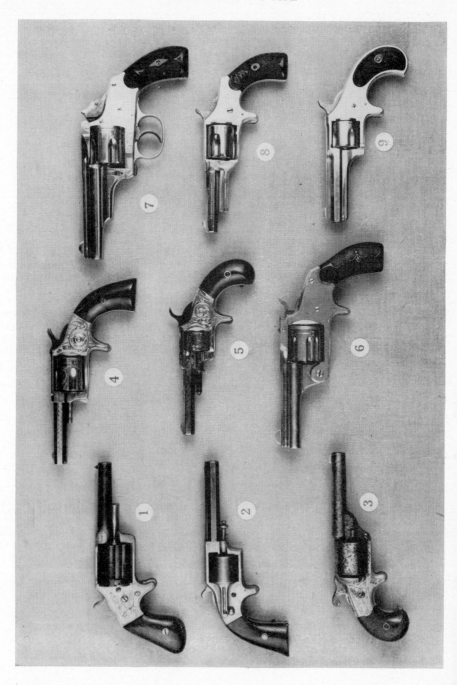

BLISS & GOODYEAR (1860-1887) New Haven, Conn.

Manufactured the following "Name Brand" S.A. solid frame revolvers: America (.32 RF with unusual 7-shot cylinder), Challenge (.32 RF), Chieftain (.32 RF), Crescent (.32 RF), Defiance (.22 RF), Excelsior (.32 RF), Nonpareil (.32 RF), Penetrator (.32 RF), Pinafore (.22 RF & .32 RF), Prairie King (.22 RF), Protector (.22 RF & .32 RF), Spy (.22 RF), True Blue (.32 RF), Winfield Arms Co. (.32 RF), Crown Jewel (.32 RF), and Veteran (.32 RF).

All the above were produced under patent of William H. Bliss dated April 23, 1878. Frank D. Bliss was the founder of this firm and made cartridge revolvers under his own patent.

BROOKLYN ARMS COMPANY (1863-1867) Brooklyn, N. Y.

Manufactured front-loading revolvers based on the F. P. Slocum patent dated April 14, 1863. Chambers are sliding tubes fitted into bores cut into cylinder. Tubes slide forward over a fixed ejector. Solid frame; single action; spur trigger.

CHRIST, ALBERT

.22 RF. 18-shot; S.A.; bottom-break; 2 superposed barrels.

Distinguishing feature: Cylinder has two concentric circles of chambers; twelve in outer circle, and six in the inner circle.

CLARK, I. J. Philadelphia, Penna.

This firm manufactured "The Improved Derringer

Figure 6. MISCELLANEOUS REVOLVERS.

1. Brooklyn Arms (Slocum) Front-loading. 2. Plant Front-loading. 3. Moore Teat-Fire. 4. Ryan "Napoleon" .32. 5. Whitneyville Armory .22. 6. American Arms Ring-Extractor .38. 7. Merwin, Hulbert .38. 8. Shattuck .32. 9. Remington New Line No. 2.

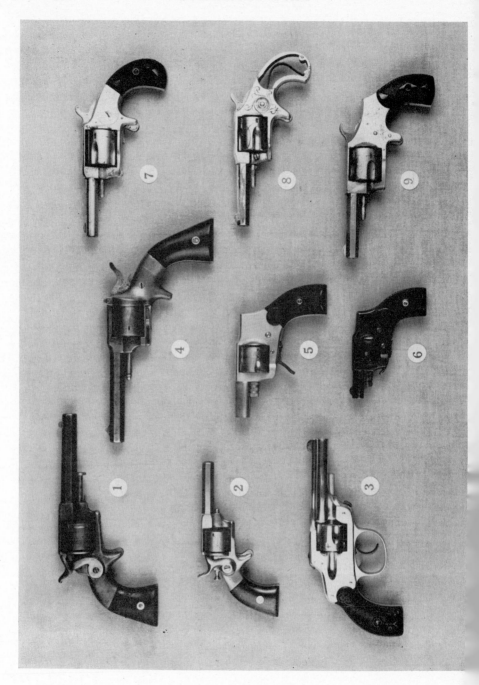

Revolver" in several sizes and calibers while the Rollin White patent was still in effect.

CODY MANUFACTURING COMPANY (1957-1959) Chicopee, Mass.

.22 RF. 6-shot; D.A.; T.B., "Thunderbird." Frame, cylinder, and barrel of aluminum—the barrel having a rifled steel liner. Steel cylinders were employed prior to discontinuance.

CONE, D. D. Washington, D.C.

Manufactured .22 RF and .32 RF single action, solid frame, sp. tr. revolvers. Identical models may be marked "W. L. Grant" or "J. P. Lower."

CONNECTICUT ARMS COMPANY (1862-1869) Norfolk, Conn.

Manufactured revolvers using teat cartridges based on S. W. Wood's patent of 1862. Front loading with attached ejector; sp. tr.; S.A.

CONTINENTAL ARMS COMPANY Norwich, Conn.

.22 RF. 7-shot; S.A.; sp. tr.; solid frame—"Continental 1."
.32 RF. 5-shot; S.A.; sp. tr.; solid frame—"Continental 2."

COPELAND, T. (1868-1874) Worcester, Mass.

.22 RF. 7-shot; S.A.; sp. tr.; solid brass frame. A 10-shot version of this revolver may be extant.

DALY ARMS COMPANY New York, N. Y.

.22 RF. 6-shot; D.A.; ring trigger.
.32 RF. 5-shot; S.A.; "Peace Maker."

It is probable that this company was a distributor rather than a manufacturer.

DARDICK CORPORATION (1959-   ) Hamden, Conn.

Manufactured a unique semi-automatic revolver firing

Figure 7. MISCELLANEOUS REVOLVERS.
1. Allen & Wheelock Side Hammer .32. 2. Allen & Wheelock Side Hammer .22. 3. Parker Safety Hammerless .32. 4. Pond "Army" .32. 5. Kolb "Baby Hammerless" .32. 6. Sedgley "Baby Hammerless" .22. 7. Bliss & Goodyear "Crown Jewel" .32. 8. Lee Arms "Red Jacket No. 3" .32. 9. Dickinson "Earthquake" .32.

cartridges called "trounds." The cylinder is continuously fed by a magazine holding up to 20 "trounds."

DERRINGER RIFLE & PISTOL WORKS Philadelphia, Penna.

.22 **RF.** 7-shot; S.A.; sp. tr.; bottom-break—"Centennial 1876."

.32 **RF.** 5-shot; S.A.; sp. tr.; bottom-break.

.38 **RF.** 5-shot; S.A.; sp. tr.; bottom-break—"Centennial 1876."

Produced in 1870's after expiration of R. White's patent.

DICKINSON, E. L. (1863-1880) Springfield, Mass.

Manufactured .32 RF, 5-shot, S.A., solid frame revolvers with brand names of Earlhood, Earthquake and Ranger No. 2. Hopkins & Allen also made a revolver with the brand name of Ranger No. 2.

EAGLE FIREARMS COMPANY (1865-1870) New York, N. Y.

Manufactured the Plant front-loading revolvers at the J. J. Marlin factory, Rock Falls, N. Y.

EASTERN ARMS COMPANY

Cartridge handguns are known bearing this marking. The firm is not verified as a manufacturer.

EMPIRE STATE ARMS COMPANY

Cartridge handguns are known bearing this marking. The firm is not verified as a manufacturer.

FIEHL & WEEKS FIRE ARMS MFG. COMPANY Philadelphia, Penna.

.32 **S&W.** 5-shot; D.A.; hammerless; "Perfect." Patented February 24, 1891.

FOREHAND & WADSWORTH (1871-1880) Worcester, Mass. (Forehand Arms Company, 1880-1902.)

This was a continuation of the Ethan Allen & Company, Ethan Allen having died in 1871. Both Forehand

and Wadsworth were sons-in-law of Ethan Allen. Wadsworth retired from business in 1880 and the company was continued as the Forehand Arms Company. Forehand died in 1898 and Hopkins & Allen absorbed the company in 1902.

.22 RF, .30 RF, .32RF, .44RF. S.A.; sp. tr.; side-hammer.

.22 RF. 7-shot; S.A.; solid frame; center-hammer.

.32 RF. 5-shot; S.A.; solid frame; sp. tr.; "Terror."

.32 RF. 5-shot; S.A.; solid frame; sp. tr.; "Russian Model-32."

.38 S&W. 6-shot; D.A.; solid frame with integral ejector rod which slides into a recess within the cylinder pin and locks the cylinder pin during firing: "British Bulldog."

.41 RF. 5-shot; S.A.; solid frame; sp. tr.; "Swamp Angel."

.44 Russian. 6-shot; S.A.; solid frame; 7½-inch barrel; known to collectors as the "Old Model Army."

.44 Russian. 6-shot; S.A.; solid frame; 6½-inch barrel; known to collectors as the "New Model Army."

Note: This firm also made double action, top-break revolvers, both hammer and hammerless styles, in the popular calibers.

FRYBERG, ANDREW & COMPANY Hopkinton, Mass.

Manufactured double action, top-break revolvers, both hammer and hammerless styles, in calibers .32 S&W and .38 S&W based on patent dated August 4, 1903.

GRANT, W. L. (See CONE, D. D.)

GREAT WESTERN GUN WORKS (1866-1895) Pittsburgh, Penna.

.22 RF. 7-shot; S.A.; sp. tr.; solid frame.

.32 RF. 5-shot; S.A.; sp. tr.; solid frame.

This firm was also a distributor for many other makes of firearms.

GROSS ARMS COMPANY (1841-1886) Tiffin, Ohio.

Manufactured cartridge handguns in calibers .22 RF, .25 RF, .32 RF.

HOOD FIRE ARMS COMPANY (1870-   ) Norwich, Conn.

Probably the largest manufacturer of single action, spur trigger, solid frame revolvers referred to as "Suicide Specials." Controlled the Norwich Arms Company and the Norwich Lock Manufacturing Company and possibly several companies making this type of handgun. The following patent dates establish Hood as the parent manufacturer: February 23, 1875, April 6, 1875. and March 14, 1876.

Virtually all Hood products bore brand names and included the following: Alexis, Alaska, Boys Choice, Brutus, Czar, Hard Pan, International, Jewel, Little John, Robin Hood, Scout, Union Jack, Victoria, Wide Awake.

All the above were either .22 RF, 7-shot, or .32 RF, 5-shot. The Alexis (.22 RF) and the Czar (.22 RF) were made for Turner & Ross, Boston, Mass.

IRVING WILLIAM (1861-1870) New York, N. Y.

Manufactured cartridge revolvers in calibers .22 RF, .30 RF, and .32 RF under the Reid Patent of April 28, 1863.

KOLB, HENRY (1892-1930) Philadelphia, Penna.

.22 RF. 6-shot; D.A.; folding trigger; "Baby Hammerless."

.32 S&W. 5-shot; D.A.; folding trigger; "Baby Hammerless."

Note: Numerous variations of this model will be found. This company was taken over by R. F. Sedgley, Inc., about 1930.

LEE ARMS COMPANY (1870's) Wilkes-Barre, Penna.

.22 RF. 7-shot; S.A.; sp. tr.; solid frame; "Red Jacket No. 1."

.32 RF. 5-shot; S.A.; sp. tr.; solid frame; "Red Jacket No. 2," "Red Jacket No. 3," "Red Jacket No. 4." No. 3 was engraved.

LOWELL ARMS COMPANY (1866-1867) Lowell, Mass. (ROLLIN WHITE ARMS CO., 1864-1866.)

.22 RF. 7-shot; S.A.; sp. tr.; solid frame; cylinder pin. Many of these were marked: "Made for Smith & Wesson." See chapter 1 for explanation.

LOWER, J. P. (See CONE, D. D.)

MALTBY, HENLEY, & COMPANY (1878-1890) New York, N. Y. (MALTBY, CORLISS & CO.)

Manufactured cartridge revolvers under the John T. Smith patent of March 11, 1884. The "Metropolitan Police" model was allegedly issued to the police force of New York.

Columbian New Safety Hammerless. .22 RF, .32 S&W, .38 S&W; D.A.; hammerless, safety lever on tang. This bears patent dates January 24, 1888, October 28, 1889, assigned to John T. Smith, Rockfall, Conn. Marked "Maltby, Henley & Co., N. Y."

Parker Safety Hammerless. .32 S&W; D.A.; hammerless; safety lever on tang.

Distinguishing feature: Cylinder stop on top-strap. Bears patent dates October 29, 1883, January 24, 1888. No other markings.

MANHATTAN FIREARMS MANUFACTURING COMPANY (1840-1870) Newark, N. J., New York (after 1864).

.22 RF. 7-shot; S.A.; sp. tr.; bottom-break similar to Smith & Wesson's No. 1.

.32 RF. 6-shot; S.A.; sp. tr.; bottom-break.

MARLIN FIREARMS COMPANY (1870-   ) New Haven, Conn.

.22 RF. 7-shot; S.A.; sp. tr.; solid frame; "Little Joker."

.22 RF. 7-shot; S.A.; sp. tr.; solid frame; "OK."

.22 RF. 7-shot; S.A.; sp. tr.; bottom-break; "XX Standard."

.30 RF. 5-shot; S.A.; sp. tr.; bottom-break; "XXX Standard."

.32 RF. 5-shot; S.A.; sp. tr.; bottom-break; "32 Standard."

.38 S&W. 5-shot; S.A.; sp. tr.; bottom-break; "38 Standard."

.44 S&W Russian. D.A.; 6-shot; cylinder swings out to the right on a split yoke solid frame. Cylinder pin also serves as extractor. Lanyard ring in butt.

Double Action—.32 S&W, .38 S&W. 5-shot; D.A.; T.B. Almost identical in appearance to earliest Smith & Wesson double action top-break revolvers, this was the last model of handgun manufactured by Marlin and was discontinued about 1900.

MERIDEN FIREARMS COMPANY (1863-1890) Meriden, Conn.

.38 S&W. 5-shot; D.A.; T.B.; hammerless.

MERWIN, HULBERT & COMPANY

It is probable that all handguns bearing this company's name were subcontracted to, and made by, other manufacturers—the principal manufacturer being Hopkins & Allen. Merwin, Hulbert & Co. took out 8 patents between January 24, 1874 and March 6, 1877 and, in addition, held patents dated April 17, 1877, June 15, 1880, March 14, 1882, and January 9, 1883.

The most distinguishing feature of their handguns is the unique assembly and disassembly—the barrel and cylinder rotating to the right and moving forward on a fixed cylinder pin for both loading and extraction. When assembled, the cylinder is completely recessed in the recoil plate.

MOHAWK ARMS COMPANY (1870's) Mohawk, N. Y.
.32 RF. 5-shot; S.A.; sp. tr.; solid frame.
Distinguishing feature: Cylinder stop in top-strap.

MOORE PATENT FIRE ARMS COMPANY (1862-1865)
Brooklyn, N. Y.
Manufactured teat-fire cartridge revolvers, single-action, under Daniel Moore's patent of September 18, 1860. Also manufactured single action revolvers using regular type .32 RF and .44 RF cartridges.

NATIONAL ARMS COMPANY (1865-1869) Brooklyn, N. Y.
This company took over the Moore Patent Fire Arms Co. and continued the manufacture of the teat-fire cartridge revolvers which loaded from the front.

NEW YORK PISTOL COMPANY (1870's) New York, N. Y.
.32 RF. 5-shot; S.A.; sp. tr.; solid frame; "Mohegan."
Controlled by the Hood Fire Arms Co. as a sales outlet.

NORTHFIELD KNIFE COMPANY Northfield, Conn.
.22 RF, .32 RF. S.A.; sp tr.; solid frame.

NORWICH ARMS COMPANY (1870's) Norwich, Conn.
.32 RF. 5-shot; S.A.; sp. tr.; solid frame.
Distinguishing feature: This model was produced with engraved frame and engraved metal grips. While Norwich Arms Co. was controlled by Hood Fire Arms Co., some of their revolvers carry a Bliss & Goodyear patent date.

NORWICH LOCK MFG. COMPANY (1870's) Norwich, Conn.
This company manufactured solid frame, spur trigger,

cartridge revolvers. This was another Hood subsidiary operation.

NORWICH PISTOL COMPANY (1870's) Norwich, Conn.

22 RF. 7-shot; S.A.; sp. tr.; solid frame. Probably another Hood subsidiary.

OSGOOD GUN WORKS (1880's) Norwich, Conn.

Duplex. .22 RF (8-shot) and .32 RF (1-shot); S.A.; sp. tr.; T.B. This revolver has two superposed barrels; the .32 barrel serving as a base pin for the .22 cylinder. The hammer has an adjustable nose for firing the lower barrel after, or before, firing the cartridges in cylinder. No ejector. Patented December 7, 1880, by Freeman W. Hood. This company was undoubtedly controlled by the patentee.

PLANT MANUFACTURING COMPANY (1860-1866) New Haven, Conn.

Army Revolver.

.42 Cup-primer. 6-shot; S.A.; sp. tr.; solid frame; hollow-base cup-primer cartridges load from the front; fixed ejector rod on right side of frame. This company also made cup-primer revolvers in cal's. .28, .30 and .36.

.22 RF. 7-shot; S.A.; sp. tr.; solid frame.

POND, L. W. (1859-1870) Worcester, Mass.

Army Revolver.

.44 RF. 6-shot; S.A.; sp. tr.; bottom-break. Classed as a secondary martial revolver.

.32 RF. 6-shot; S.A.; sp. tr.; bottom-break.

The above two revolvers were infringements of the R. White patent held by Smith & Wesson and their manufacture was discontinued by legal action in 1863.

.22 RF. 7-shot; S.A.; sp. tr.; solid frame.

.32 RF. 6-shot; S.A.; sp. tr.; solid frame.

The above two revolvers were loaded from the front

via separate-chamber sleeves which could be withdrawn to the front for loading or extraction of cartridge cases. Rotating ejector rod is attached to base pin. Rear of cylinder has slots at each chamber for firing nose of hammer. These revolvers evaded the R. White patent and were manufactured from 1863 until sometime after the Civil War.

PRESCOTT, E. A. (1860-1863) Worcester, Mass.
Navy Revolver.
.38 RF. 6-shot; S.A.; solid frame; trigger guard with finger-rest spur. A secondary martial cartridge revolver.
.32 RF. 6-shot; S.A.; solid frame; sp. tr.
.22 RF. 7-shot; S.A.; solid frame; sp. tr.
The above .22 and .32 were of similar design as the "Navy" with the exception of having spur triggers.
.22 RF. 7-shot; S.A.; sp. tr.; solid frame.
.32 RF. 6-shot; S.A.; sp. tr.; solid frame.
The above two revolvers closely resemble Smith & Wesson's No. 1, second issue, and No. 2 "Army" respectively, with the exception that they do not break at bottom. Prescott also made another model of .22 and .32 RF revolver of solid frame with bird-head grips.

PROTECTOR ARMS COMPANY Philadelphia, Penna.
.22 RF. S.A.; 7-shot; sp. tr.; solid frame. "Protector Arms Co." was a trade name used by the Rupertus Patent Pistol Mfg. Co.

REID, JAMES (1862-1884) New York, N.Y., Catskill, N.Y.
.22 RF. 7-shot; S.A.; sp. tr.
.41 RF. 5-shot; S.A.; sp. tr.; solid frame; metal grips.
.32 RF or **.31 Percussion.** 6-shot; S.A., sp. tr. Patented April 28, 1863, this revolver was designed to convert from percussion to cartridge, or vice versa.
.41 RF. 5-shot; S.A.; sp. tr.; solid frame; metal grips.
Distinguishing features: Narrow bow extending from

trigger sheath to base of butt; hammer spur rounded-stub.

Note: Reid's "Knuckledusters" are covered under chapter 5.

ROLLIN WHITE ARMS COMPANY (1858-1866) Lowell, Mass.
.22 RF. 7-shot; S.A.; sp. tr.; solid frame.

Distinguishing features: Many marked "Made for Smith & Wesson"—see chapter 1.

Note: Company name changed to Lowell Arms Company in 1866.

ROME REVOLVER & NOVELTY WORKS (187?-188?) Rome, N.Y.
.32 RF. 5-shot; S.A.; sp. tr.; solid frame.

RUPERTUS PATENT PISTOL MFG. COMPANY (1858-1888) Philadelphia, Penna.
.22 RF. 7-shot; S.A.; sp. tr.; solid frame; "Empire."
.38 RF. 5-shot; S.A.; sp. tr.; solid frame; "Empire" or "Empire No. 1."
.41 RF. 5-shot; S. A.; sp. tr.; solid frame; "Empire 41."

RYAN, THOMAS E. MFG. COMPANY (1870-1876?) Norwich, Conn. (RYAN PISTOL MFG. CO.) New York, N.Y.
.22 RF. 7-shot; S.A.; sp. tr.; solid frame; "T.E. Ryan Mfg. Co."
.32 RF. 5-shot; S.A.; sp. tr.; solid frame; "Ryan's New Model."
.22 RF. 7-shot; S.A.; sp. tr.; solid frame; "Napoleon."
.32 RF. 5-shot; S.A.; sp. tr.; solid frame; "Napoleon."

SCOTT ARMS COMPANY
.32 RF. 5-shot; S.A.; sp. tr.; solid frame; "Pat. 1878."

Note: "Scott Arms Co." probably was a trade-name rather than that of a manufacturer.

SEDGLEY, R. F., INC. (1930-   ) Philadelphia, Penna.
.22 RF. 6-shot; D.A.; folding trigger; "Baby Hammer-less." This pocket revolver was advertised as a "Garter Pistol" and will be found in several model variations. Sedgley took over production of this model from Kolb about 1930.

SHATTUCK ARMS COMPANY (1879-19   ) Hatfield, Mass.
.32 RF. 5-shot; S.A.; sp. tr.; solid frame. Cylinder swings out to right of frame on cylinder pin which is pivoted to frame extension under barrel; extraction accomplished by pushing forward on cylinder; cylinder latch on recoil plate, right.
.38 RF. 5-shot; S.A.; sp. tr.; solid frame; (same as above). These 2 revolvers were patented November 4, 1879.

SMITH ARMS COMPANY New York, N.Y.
.32 (uses an odd cartridge with primer in a belted rim). Based on Crispin's patent of October 3, 1865.

SMITH, OTIS A. (1873-1890) Rockfall, Conn.
.22 RF. 7-shot; S.A.; sp. tr.; solid frame; "No. 22."
.32 RF. 5-shot; S.A.; sp. tr.; solid frame; "No. 32."
.38 RF. 5-shot; S.A.; sp tr.; solid frame; "No. 38."
.41 RF. 5-shot; S.A.; sp. tr.; solid frame; "No. 41."
  Distinguishing feature: Section of cylinder pin within cylinder actuated to rear by spring pressure of forward section of cylinder pin.
  Note: The above revolvers were based on O.A. Smith's patent of April 15, 1873.
.32 S&W. 5-shot; S.A.; T.B.; sp. tr; thumb ejector; floating firing pin; "Model 1883 Shell Ejector" Pat. December 20, 1881.

SPRINGFIELD ARMS COMPANY (1851-1869) Springfield, Mass.
.32 RF. 5-shot; S.A.; sp. tr.; brass frame. As these were

an infringement of the R. White patent, some specimens may be marked "Mfg. for Smith & Wesson."

STANDARD REVOLVER COMPANY

This company manufactured bottom-break cartridge revolvers similar in design to the early Smith & Wesson models. J. M. Marlin took over the company in the early 1880's and continued manufacture of "Standard" revolvers.

THAMES ARMS COMPANY Norwich, Conn.

.22 RF. 7-shot; D.A.; T.B.

.32 S&W. 5-shot; D.A.; T.B.

.38 S&W. 5-shot; D.A.; T.B.

TURNER & ROSS

Not a manufacturer but a distributor, or agent. Handguns bearing this name were contracted and may not all have been made by any one company.

U. M. C. ARMS COMPANY

.32 RF. 5-shot; S.A.; sp. tr.; "Pat. April 23, '79." This may have been a subsidiary, or trade-name, of another manufacturer.

UNION FIREARMS COMPANY (1900-190?) Toledo, Ohio

.32 S&W, .38 S&W. This company made "semi-automatic" revolvers in above calibers designed to utilize recoil for rotating cylinder and cocking hammer following initial discharge.

UNITED STATES ARMS COMPANY (1870-1878) Brooklyn, N.Y.

.22 RF. 7-shot; S.A.; sp. tr.; solid frame.

.32 RF. 6-shot; S.A.; sp. tr.; solid frame; "No. 32."

.38 RF. 5-shot; S.A.; sp. tr.; solid frame; "No. 38."

.41 RF. 5-shot; S.A.; sp. tr.; solid frame; "No. 41."

Distinguishing feature: Double-blade pincer type cylinder pin release.

U.S. REVOLVER CO. Fitchburg, Mass.

This was a trade-name employed by the Iver Johnson Arms & Cycle Works who were the manufacturers. Handguns were made with this marking from 1910-1930.

WARNER, JAMES (1851-1866) Springfield, Mass.

.30 RF. 5-shot; S.A.; tr. guard; loading gate—"Warner's Patent 1857." This revolver was an infringement of the R. White patent.

WESSON & HARRINGTON (1871-1874) Worcester, Mass.

.22 RF. 7-shot; S.A.; sp. tr.; solid frame; "Shell-Ejector."

.32 RF. 5-shot; S.A.; sp. tr.; solid frame; "Shell-Ejector."

.38 RF. 5-shot; S.A.; sp. tr.; solid frame; "Shell-Ejector."

Note: These were the first American cartridge revolvers to incorporate integral ejector rod, thus eliminating the necessity of removing cylinder to eject cartridge cases. Wesson & Harrington also produced standard solid frame revolvers without ejector rod. Wesson & Harrington became Harrington & Richardson in 1874 and this firm is still in business.

WESTERN ARMS COMPANY (1860's) Chicago and New York.

.32 RF. Folding trigger.

Note: This company may have been a distributor only, rather than a manufacturer.

WHITNEY ARMS COMPANY (1841-1888) Whitneyville, Conn. (WHITNEYVILLE ARMORY)

.22 RF. 7-shot; S.A.; sp. tr.; solid frame—"Pat. May 23, 1871."

.32 RF. 5-shot; S.A.; sp. tr.; solid frame—"Pat. May 23, 1871."

.38 RF. 5-shot; S.A.; sp. tr.; solid frame—sometimes referred to as "House Model."

WRIGHT ARMS COMPANY (1870's) Lawrence, Mass.

.22 RF. 5-shot; D.A.; folding trigger or "pull" in tube above barrel; solid frame; cylinder pin fixes cylinder. This is a "squeezer" type revolver. The trigger, or "pull," folds down over muzzle of barrel when not in use to prevent entry of foreign substances into barrel. This palm pistol was hammerless and was named "Little All Right." It was patented January 18, 1876.

CHAPTER 4

Single Shot Pistols

Single shot pistols enjoyed a great vogue during the early years of the cartridge era but have long since all but vanished from the American scene. In mid-1959, there was but one American-made single shot pistol on the market—the Sheridan "Knocabout." Since then Savage has reentered the handgun field from which they had long been absent with a single shot .22 cal. pistol and Colt has brought out two single shot models in .22 cal.—see chapter 8.

Single shot pistols were cheaper to make than revolvers and could be had in pocket sizes of very light weight. Because they were small and cheap, many who desired personal protection chose to carry a pair of single shots rather than one revolver.

Single shot pistols were also once in demand as target pieces. They are generally conceded to be more accurate than revolvers inasmuch as the cartridge is chambered directly in the barrel rather than in a cylinder chamber, thus eliminating bullet-jump, possible shaving of the bullet as it enters the barrel and attendant loss of gas. But modern competitive pistol matches in America call for timed and rapid as well as slow-fire. This virtually necessitates the use of a revolver or semi-automatic pistol and has sounded the death-knell for the single shot as a target arm. The single shot has little place in the America of today other than as a "plinker," trap-line gun, weapon for killing farm animals or conversation piece.

ALLEN, ETHAN & COMPANY Worcester, Mass.

.**41 RF.** Sp tr.; Derr.; center hung hammer; Allen's Pat. March 7, 1865; barrel swings to side to load. (Resembles Colt's No. 3 Deringer.) Also made in .32 RF.

ALLEN & WHEELOCK Worcester, Mass.

.**22 RF.** Sp. tr., Derr.

.**32 RF.** Sp. tr.; Derr.

.**41 RF.** Sp. tr.; Derr.

BABCOCK

.**32 RF.** Sp tr.; "Babcock's Patent."

BACON MANUFACTURING COMPANY Norwich, Conn.

.**32 RF.** Sp. tr.; iron frame; barrel swings right to load; 4-inch barrel (not a Derr.).

BALLARD, C. H. & COMPANY Worcester, Mass.

.**41 RF.** Sp. tr.; Derr.; barrel-breech tips up to load.

BROWN MANUFACTURING COMPANY Newbury-port, Mass.

.**41 RF.** Sp. tr.; Derr.; barrel swings to side to load; "Southerner" Pat. April 9, 1867.

Note: Brown Mfg. Co. absorbed the Merrimac Arms & Mfg. Co.

COLT'S PATENT FIRE ARMS MANUFACTURING CO. Hartford, Conn.

No. 1 Deringer.* .41 RF; sp. tr.; all metal including grip, flat-top barrel revolves left to load; button breech lock release on right of frame; engraved.

No. 2 Deringer. .41 RF; sp. tr.; engraved frame, wood grips; flat-top barrel revolves left to load; button breech lock release on right of frame.

Note: Colt's No. 1 and 2 Deringers were previously manufactured by National Arms Company and are at

---

* Spelling used by manufacturer.

times referred to as Colt's "National" Deringers. (Also see note under Moore Patent Fire Arms Company.)

No. 3 Deringer. .41 RF; sp. tr.; plain frame, wood grips; barrel-breech swings right to load; round barrel; snap-type breech lock; automatic ejector. Colt designated this model the "New Patent Deringer" but it is also referred to as the "Thuer" deringer, having been designed by an official of Colt's of this name.

Camp Perry Model. .22 RF; barrel integral with block replacing cylinder swings out left to load and eject via extractor pin under barrel; same grip and trigger position as Officers' Model revolver; first issued with 10-inch barrel, action (hammer fall) shortened and barrel reduced to 8-inches in 1933; target sights; discontinued in 1941.

No. 4 Deringer. .22 RF (Short); sp. tr.; a replica in .22 caliber of the Colt No. 3 Deringer. Available with gold-plated frame, blued barrel and wood grips, or entirely nickle-plated with imitation ivory grips. Introduced in 1959.

Civil War Centennial Model. .22 RF (Short); scaled down replica in .22 caliber of Colt's 1860 Army percussion revolver. Dummy "cylinder" and "loading lever" are non-functional. Introduced in 1961.

CONNECTICUT ARMS & MANUFACTURING CO.
Naubuc, Conn.

.44 RF. (Henry). "Hammond Bull Dog" Pat. October 25, 1864. Breech block revolves left with release on top of frame; sp. tr.

.41 RF. Same as above.

CONTINENTAL ARMS COMPANY Norwich, Conn.

.22 RF. Sp. tr.; hammer acts as breech block.

COWLES & SMITH (COWLES & SON) Chicopee, Mass.

.22 RF. Sp. tr.; barrel swings right to load; brass frame.

CRESCENT FIRE ARMS COMPANY Norwich, Conn.

.410 Gauge. Lever on tang permits breech to break up as in single barrel shotguns.

DICKINSON, E. L. & J. Springfield, Mass.

.32 RF. Sp. tr.; brass frame; manually-operated rack-and-pinion extractor under barrel.

.22 RF. Same as above.

DRISCOLE, J. B. Springfield, Mass.

.22 RF. Sp. tr.; bronze frame; breech tips up to load.

ELLIS, WILLARD C. Springfield, Mass.

.32 RF. Sp. tr.; Pat. April, 1859.

FOREHAND & WADSWORTH Worcester, Mass.

.41 RF. Sp. tr.; Derr.

HARRINGTON & RICHARDSON Worcester, Mass.

.22 RF. T.B.; automatic ejector; adjustable target sights; trigger guard with finger rest spur; one piece walnut grip. Standard barrel length, 10-inches—also available in 7-inch and 8-inch lengths. Designated "U.S.R.A. Model," this single shot arm is known to exist in at least two issues differing principally in type of automatic ejector employed—a flip-type flat lever, or a tubular plunger.

Handygun. .410 ga., 28 ga., .22 RF, .32-20 WCF.

Note: The "Handygun" is designed much as a single barrel shotgun, a lever on tang breaking the barrel breech upwards. The handle is one-piece checkered walnut with short fore-end screwed to barrel. Best known in .410 version, it was available in other gauges or calibers as above. The two gauges were available in both 8-inch and 12¼-inch barrel lengths while the two calibers were available in 12¼-inch barrel length only.

HARTFORD ARMS & EQUIPMENT COMPANY Hartford, Conn.

.22 RF. Frame and action resembles early High Standard semi-automatic pistols; drawing slide back cocks hammer and opens breech for loading; slide and breech block is locked during discharge and must be released by lever on left side of frame.

Note: Hartford Arms & Equip. Co. was bought by the High Standard Manufacturing Corporation in 1932.

HIGH STANDARD MANUFACTURING CORPORATION Hamden, Conn.

Note: This firm developed a "Free Pistol" for the 1960 Olympic pistol team which incorporated a battery-operated sear release. It has not been made available commercially.

HOPKINS & ALLEN Norwich, Conn.

.22 RF. Folding trigger; barrel breech tips up to load; engraved frame; Derr.; sometimes called "Ladies Garter Pistol."

.22 RF. T.B.; 10-inch barrel; "New Model Target Pistol."

.41 RF. "XL Derringer."

IVER JOHNSON ARMS & CYCLE WORKS Fitchburg, Mass.

.22 RF. Sp. tr.; barrel swings to side to load; Derr.

.32 RF. Sp. tr.; barrel swings to side to load; Derr.

Note: Above models designated "Star Vest Pocket" and "Eclipse." These were the first pistols of this design to employ .22 and .32 rimfire cartridges.

LOMBARD, H. C. & COMPANY Springfield, Mass.

.22 RF, .32 RF. Sp. tr.; brass frame; barrel swings to side to load; plunger breech release under frame.

MARLIN FIREARMS COMPANY New Haven, Conn.

.22 RF. Sp. tr.; barrel swings to right to load; "Vest Pocket."

.22 RF. Sp. tr.; barrel swings to right to load; "OK."

.22 RF, .32 RF, .41 RF. Sp. tr.; barrel swings to side to load; "Never Miss" series.

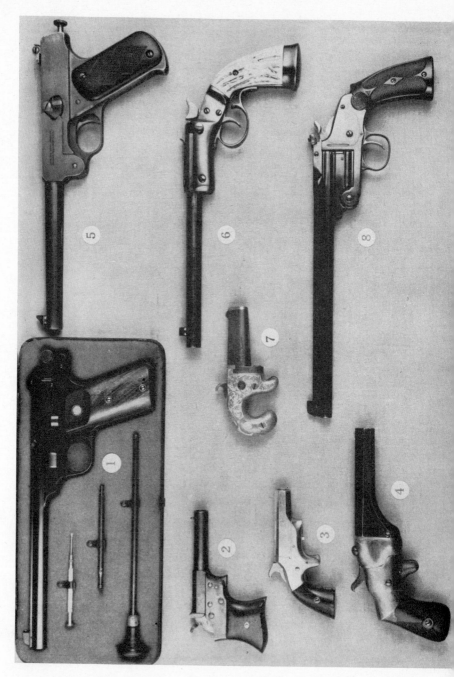

.38 RF. Sp. tr.; barrel swings to side to load; "Victor."

Note: All above Marlin derringers had a plunger breech release under frame.

MERRIMAC ARMS & MANUFACTURING COMPANY Newburyport, Mass.

.41 RF. Sp. tr.; barrel swings to side to load—"Southerner." Patented April 9, 1867.

Note: This derringer was continued by the Brown Manufacturing Co. after they absorbed the Merrimac Arms & Manufacturing Co.

MOORE PATENT FIRE ARMS COMPANY Brooklyn, N. Y.

.41 RF. Sp. tr.; barrel revolves left to load; one-piece metal frame and handle; flat-top barrel. D. Moore's Pat. February 24, 1863.

Note: This derringer was continued substantially unchanged by the National Arms Company who absorbed the Moore Patent Fire Arms Co. in 1865. The Moore derringer was also produced in .38 RF.

MORGAN & CLAPP New Haven, Conn.

.22 RF, .30 RF, .32 RF. Sp. tr.; brass frame; barrel swings right to load.

NATIONAL ARMS COMPANY Brooklyn, N. Y.

.41 RF. Sp. tr.; barrel revolves left to load; one piece metal frame and handle; flat-top barrel; "No. 1 Derringer."

.41 RF. "No. 2 Derringer," grips made of wood and differing in shape from the No. 1.

REMINGTON ARMS COMPANY Bridgeport, Conn.

.22 RF, .32 RF, .38 RF, .41 RF. Sp. tr.; irregular square

Figure 8. SINGLE SHOT PISTOLS.
1. Smith & Wesson "Straight Line," cased. 2. Remington Vest Pocket Derringer .41. 3. Merrimac "Southerner" Derringer .41. 4. Connecticut Arms "Hammond Bulldog" .44. 5. Stevens "Target," Model 10. 6. Stevens "Off-Hand," Model 35. 7. Moore Derringer .41. 8. Smith & Wesson Model of 1891, 2nd Issue.

butt, wood grips; hammer acts as striker and breech block; Elliot's pat. October 1, 1861, November 15, 1864. "Vest Pocket Derringer."

.41 RF. Sp. tr.; bird-head grip; Elliot's pat. August 27, 1867. "Remington-Elliot Derringer."

.50 RF. Sp. tr.; rolling-block action; 8½-inch barrel; "Model 1866 Navy."

.50 CF. Regulation trigger and trigger guard; rolling-block action; 7-inch barrel; "Model 1867 Navy."

.50 CF. Regulation trigger and trigger guard; rolling-block action; 8-inch barrel; "Model 1871 Army."

.22 RF; .44 S&W Russian. Rolling-block action, 8-inch and 10-inch barrel; "Model 1891 Target."

.22 RF; .44 S&W Russian. Rolling-block action; 8-inch and 10-inch barrel; "Model 1901 Target" (refined de luxe version of Model 1891).

ROLLIN WHITE ARMS COMPANY Lowell, Mass.

.32 RF, .38 RF. Sp. tr.; chamber rotates out of frame to load. Patented April 13, 1858.

RUPERTUS PATENT PISTOL MFG. COMPANY Philadelphia, Penna.

.22 RF, .32 RF, .38 RF. Sp. tr.; iron frame; barrel revolves left to load.

SAVAGE ARMS CORPORATION Westfield, Mass.

Model 101 Single Action Safety Single Shot. .22 RF; barrel and dummy "cylinder" are integral and swing as a unit to right for loading and extraction. Fixed slide-extractor rod. Introduced in 1959.

SHERIDAN PRODUCTS, INC. Racine, Wisc.

Model D. Knocabout. .22 RF; safety on left of frame;

Figure 9. SINGLE SHOT PISTOLS.

1. Harrington & Richardson "Handygun" .410 ga. 2. Hartford Arms .22. 3. Savage Model 101 Safety .22. 4. Sheridan "Knocabout" Model D .22. 5. Harrington & Richardson "Model U.S.R.A." .22. 6. Wamo "Powermaster" .22. 7. S-M "Sporter" .22. 8. Marlin "OK" Derringer .22.

barrel breech tips up to load; automatic ejector; breech-release forward of trigger guard; coil mainspring; floating firing pin; brown plastic grips. Introduced in 1953.

S-M (Sydney Manson) CORP. Alexandria, Va.

S-M Sporter. .22 RF; bolt action; blow back ejection; safety lever and bolt release left side of frame; one piece black plastic stock. Introduced about 1953 (obsolete).

SMITH & WESSON Springfield, Mass.

Model of 1891, First Issue. Single shot barrels in calibers .22 RF, .32 S&W, and .38 S&W could be mounted on the frame of the Model of 1891 S.A., T.B. revolver, thus converting it into a single shot target pistol. These single shot barrels were available in 6-inch, 8-inch, and 10-inch lengths.

Model of 1891, Second Issue. .22 RF; S.A.; T.B.; 10-inch barrel; Model of 1891 S.A. revolver frame without recoil plate, cylinder stop slot, or hand slot. First exclusively single shot Smith & Wesson pistol.

Perfected Target Pistol. .22 RF; D.A.; T.B.; 10-inch barrel; designed along lines of the .38 S&W D.A. "Perfected" revolver.

Model Straight Line. .22 RF; S.A.; 10-inch barrel; hammer-striker draws straight back to cock and has half-cock; frame resembles that of a semi-automatic pistol; release latch on left side of frame permits breech end of barrel to swing right on pivot; straight trigger pull.

STAFFORD, T. J. New Haven, Conn.

.22 RF. Brass frame; sp. tr.

STARR ARMS COMPANY New York, N. Y.

.38 RF; .41 RF. Brass frame; button trigger, side hammer; barrel breech tips up to load; Starr's Pat. May 10, 1864.

STEVENS, J. ARMS COMPANY Chicopee Falls, Mass.

Kick-Up. .22 RF. Trigger extends forward of frame

below barrel recess; irregular-shaped "fish-tail" grips; barrel breech springs up for loading. Made in other calibers.

Gem. .22 RF, .30 RF. Very similar to the Marlin "OK."

Gould—Conlin—Lord. These were heavy frame target pistols. Barrel breech tips up to load. Button barrel catch release on left side of frame. Various barrel lengths and calibers.

Diamond Model 43 Target Pistol. .22 RF; light frame; barrel breech tips up to load; barrel catch release on left side of frame; several barrel lengths.

Tip Up Model 41. .22 RF; light frame; barrel breech tips up to load; barrel catch release on left side of frame; flat butt.

Off-Hand Target Pistol Model 35. .22 RF; medium weight frame; barrel-breech tips up to load; barrel catch release on left side of frame. Made in various barrel lengths and calibers. Metal butt of frame extends below grip panels.

Target Model 10. .22 RF; heavy frame resembles that of a semi-automatic pistol; straight-pull knob cocks internal hammer; an eccentric latch under spring tension on the left side of the frame permits the breech to raise up when released and the cartridge extractor to function. Pat. April 27, 1920.

TAYLOR, L. B. & COMPANY Chicopee Falls, Mass.

.32 RF. Brass frame; sp. tr.

UNITED STATES ARMS COMPANY Brooklyn, N. Y.

.22 RF Knife Pistol. 1¼-inch barrel with attached knife blade.

VARSITY MANUFACTURING COMPANY, Springfield, Mass.

Tompkins Target Pistol. .22 RF; 8-inch barrel; one-piece stock extending from butt to muzzle. Introduced 1947 (obsolete).

WAMO MANUFACTURING COMPANY, San Gabriel, Calif.

   Powermaster Match Pistol. .22 RF; bolt action; automatic ejection accomplished via the blow-back principle which frees a flat spring under tension beneath the bolt when the bolt is forward in firing position. There is a knob on the left side of the bolt for manual operation. No safety when striker is cocked and bolt fully forward.

WESSON, FRANKLIN Worcester, Mass.

   .22 RF. Brass frame; sp. tr.; barrel breech tips up to load; the barrel catch release lever extends down from the barrel recess of the frame and forward of trigger. Patented October 25, 1859, November 11, 1862.

WURFFLEIN, WILLIAM Philadelphia, Penna.

   .22 RF. Trigger guard with finger rest spur; 10-inch barrel; barrel-breech tips up to load. Patented June 24, 1884.

CHAPTER 5

Multiple Shot Pistols

Multiple shot pistols include all handguns featuring more than one barrel with a separate barrel for each cartridge, or number of shots, which they are capable of firing. The barrel cluster may resemble an elongated revolver cylinder and in the cases of some types of pepperboxes (Bacon, Continental, Reid, Rupertus) the barrel clusters do revolve. In other types of pepperboxes (Mossberg "Brownie," Remington-Elliot, Sharps) the barrel clusters are stationary and the firing mechanism revolves.

Multiple shot pistols were never manufactured in great quantity but are among the most fascinating of all American firearms and are highly regarded by the gun collecting fraternity. From a firearms curiosa standpoint, they are as unique and cleverly fabricated as any handguns employing cartridges.

The great majority of multiple shot pistols were made, ostensibly at least, for one purpose—personal protection. Most are derringer type and inaccurate beyond normal room range. Their concealability, plus the advantages of more than one shot, undoubtedly appealed to males who faced the threat of physical danger as well as to females who might be subject to assault.

AMERICAN ARMS COMPANY Boston, Mass.

.41 RF. Sp. tr.; brass frame; 2 barrels superposed.

Distinguishing feature: Both barrels rifled in solid block, position reversed via rotation, barrel latch bottom of frame forward of spur trigger. Based on Henry F.

Wheeler's patents of October 31, 1865; June 19, 1866.
.32 RF. Sp. tr.; brass frame; 2 barrels superposed.
.22 RF—.32 RF. Sp tr.; brass frame; 2 barrels superposed.

BACON MANUFACTURING COMPANY Norwich, Conn.
.22 RF. Sp. tr.; 6-shot pepperbox; iron frame.

Distinguishing feature: Round fluted cylinder-barrels unit.

CHICAGO FIRE ARMS COMPANY Chicago, Ill.
.32 RF Extra Short. 7-shot; "The Protector."

Distinguishing feature: Circular frame containing turret-like cylinder inside; loaded by removing sideplate, or cap; revolves, cocks, and fires by squeezing external lever against frame; no conventional trigger. This type handgun is referred to as a "squeezer" or "palm pistol."

Note: This palm pistol was actually manufactured by the Ames Sword Company, Chicopee, Mass. Patented in the United States by Jacques Turbiaux (France), March 6, 1883, and by Peter H. Finnegan, August 29, 1893.

CONTINENTAL ARMS COMPANY Norwich, Conn.
.22 RF. 5-shot pepperbox; sp. tr.; iron frame; "Ladies' Companion."

Distinguishing feature: Round fluted cylinder-barrels unit.

FIALA ARMS COMPANY New York, N. Y.
.22 RF. 10-shot; frame design similar to that of a semi-automatic pistol; magazine holding cartridges slides into handle of frame.

Note: This is technically a magazine pistol—the breechblock slide must be manually released and operated to feed cartridges from the magazine into the chamber, to extract fired cartridge cases and to cock the firing mechanism. A 20-inch barrel and detachable stock were available for this pistol which converted it into a rifle.

MARBLE ARMS CORPORATION Gladstone, Mich.

.22 RF—.410 Ga. 2 barrels superposed, upper .22 cal., lower .410 ga.; detachable stock for converting to rifle; "Game Getter." Manufactured with 12-inch, 15-inch and 18-inch barrels. Striker on hammer nose adjustable for either barrel.

MARSTON, W. W. (MARSTON & KNOX) New York, N.Y.

.22 RF. 3 integral superposed barrels; sp. tr. Barrel group is hinged at bottom of frame, breaks at top. Some models fitted with 3-inch sliding daggers in grooves on left side of barrel group. Patented May 26, 1857.

.32 RF. Same as above.

.32 RF Improved 1864 Model. Has three-pronged extractor on right side of frame which must be manually operated when barrel group is broken open; no sliding dagger.

Note: The 3 barrels are fired in ascending order by a firing pin which moves upward with the cocking of the hammer. There is a round turning piece, just ahead of the hammer which is marked from 0 to 3 and has a pointer which indicates how many barrels have been fired. After loading, the disc is turned with pointer at 0.

MINNEAPOLIS FIRE ARMS COMPANY Minneapolis, Minn.

.32 RF Extra Short. 7-shot; "The Protector."

Note: This rotary magazine palm pistol, or "squeezer," is very similar to the Chicago Fire Arms Co. models and is marked with the same patent dates. See descriptive data under heading CHICAGO FIRE ARMS COMPANY.

MOSSBERG, O. F. & SONS New Haven, Conn.

.22 RF. 4-shot; D.A. pepperbox, "Brownie." Patented

July 27, 1920. Discontinued in 1932.

Distinguishing feature: Resembles pocket size semi-automatic pistol in design; barrel block is square with two parallel barrels above and two below; trigger guard is integral with barrel group and breaks from top forward when released by safety catch at rear of frame above grip; rotating eccentric firing pin in breechblock contacts cartridge rims in each chamber successively; three-inch steel strip housed vertically in frame serves as extractor.

.22 RF. 4-shot; D.A. pepperbox dubbed "Novelty" pistol by factory, but not so marked. Patented December 4, 1906. Patent and manufacturing rights sold to C. S. Shattuck in 1909.

Distinguishing feature: Barrel block is square with two parallel barrels above and two below; barrel group hinged at bottom to frame and breaks from top when released by barrel catch; revolving eccentric firing pin in breechblock of frame actuated by squeezing trigger mechanism in and out of frame; entirely metal and unmarked except for serial number.

OSGOOD GUN WORKS Norwich, Conn.

.22 RF (8-shot); **.32 RF** (1-shot). 2 barrels superposed; "Duplex."

Note: Since this multiple shot pistol is primarily a revolver, it is listed and described in chapter 3.

PERRY & GODDARD New York, N.Y.

Note: These two men were general gunsmiths and dealers who acted as agents for Sharps four-barrel cartridge pistols. They should not be mistaken as the manu-

---

Figure 10. MULTIPLE SHOT PISTOLS.

1. F. Wesson Superposed .32. 2. Remington-Rider Magazine Pistol .32. 3. Bacon Pepperbox .22. 4. Sharps Pepperbox .22. 5. Remington-Elliot Ring Trigger Pepperbox .22. 6. Great Western Double Derringer .38 Spl. 7. Reid "My Friend" Knuckleduster .22. 8. Mossberg "Brownie" Pepperbox .22.

facturers of such pistols even though marked with their names.

REID, JAMES New York, N.Y., Catskill, N.Y.

.22 RF. 7-shot; sp. tr. sheathed in one-piece solid metal frame; S.A.; hole in front of frame permitted exit of bullets from chambers; patented December 26, 1865; "My Friend." Engraved frame, brass or iron.

.32 RF. 5-shot; (same as above) "My Friend."

.41 RF. 5-shot; S.A.; one-piece bow-shaped frame as above; "J. Reid's Derringer."

Note: The patent of December 26, 1865, provided only for the formation of a ring in the all-metal frame and a sliding safety catch under the frame which locked the cylinder with chambers at midpoint of alignment with hammer and bullet exit hole in frame preventing accidental discharge.

These cartridge pepperboxes were dual-purpose handguns and are known to handgun collectors as "Knuckledusters." The circular brass frames were designed so that they could serve as brass knuckles should the occasion necessitate.

Approximately 17,000 of these "Knuckledusters" were made, the majority being of .22 caliber while only about 300 of the .41 caliber derringers were produced. The special safety which formed part of the basic patent was abandoned after production had reached about the 10,000 mark.

REMINGTON ARMS COMPANY Ilion, N.Y., Bridgeport, Conn.

.22 RF. 6-shot; D.A.; ring trigger, "Zig-Zag."

Note: Described more fully under REMINGTON, chapter 2.

.22 RF. 5-shot; D.A.; ring trigger, "Remington-Elliot Derringer." Round barrel cluster, stationary.

.32 RF. 4-shot; D.A.; ring trigger, "Rem.-Elliot Derr." Square barrel cluster, stationary.

Note: The above two derringers, or pepperboxes, were patented by William H. Elliot, May 29, 1860, October 1, 1861. They were introduced in 1863 and discontinued in 1888. The ring trigger must be pushed forward and then pulled back to actuate the firing mechanism. A revolving firing pin in breechblock contacts cartridge rims in each chamber successively. Barrel cluster breaks up for loading or extraction when catch forward of ring trigger is released. It is significant to note that the chambers in these pepperboxes are counterbored for the cartridge rims, thus permitting breech and breechblock to be flush.

.41 RF. 2-shot; S.A.; sp. tr.; 2 barrels superposed; based on Elliot's Pat., December 12, 1865; for a vertically oscillating firing pin—"Double-Derringer."

Distinguishing feature: When release lever on right side of frame is rotated 180 degrees, barrels break up from bottom on hinge above breechblock of frame.

Note: This famous "Double-Derringer" is unequivocally the best known of all Remington handguns. It was manufactured over a longer period than any other Remington handgun and its discontinuance marked the end of handgun manufacturing by this firm. Introduced in 1866, it was produced continuously up to 1935. Specimens may be marked "E. Remington & Sons" (1866-1888), "Remington Arms Co." (1888-1910), or "Remington Arms-U.M.C. Co." (1910-1935).

.32 RF Extra Short. 5-shot; S.A.; sp. tr.; Rider's Pat. August 15, 1871, "Remington-Rider Magazine Pistol."

Distinguishing feature: Tubular magazine under barrel extends almost to muzzle; entire mechanism is operated by breechblock lever which must be depressed, drawn to rear and released. Manufactured from 1871-1888.

RUPERTUS PATENT PISTOL MANUFACTURING CO. Philadelphia, Penna.

.22 RF. 2-shot; S.A.; sp. tr.; 2 barrels side by side revolve left to load; "Rupertus Double-Barrel Pistol."

Distinguishing feature: Hammer has knob-actuated movable firing pin so that either barrel may be fired first.

.22 RF. 8-shot; S.A.; sp. tr.; 8-chambered cylinder-barrel "Rupertus Pepperbox." Pat. July 19, 1864.

Distinguishing feature: Novel breech plate revolves to left when hammer is at half-cock, exposing loading gate and blocking hammer fall while loading. The eight bores have slight degree of convergence toward muzzle.

SHARPS, C. & COMPANY (1854-1874) Philadelphia, Penna. **SHARPS & HANKINS** (1862-1866).

.22 RF. 4-shot; S.A.; sp. tr.; 4 barrels, top 2 parallel and bottom 2 parallel; barrel group slides forward from breechblock when released by either a plunger located forward under frame near muzzles or by a button type release located on left side of frame near breech.

Distinguishing feature: Ratchet on hammer revolves firing pin on hammer nose each time it is cocked, permitting barrels to be fired in rotation.

.30 RF. 4-shot; S.A.; sp. tr.; (same as above).

.32 RF. 4-shot; S.A.; sp. tr.; (same as above).

Note: The above 4-barreled pepperboxes, or derringers, were patented by C. Sharps, January 25, 1859, and may be marked either "C. Sharps Patent 1859" or "Address Sharps & Hankins, Philadelphia, Penna." depending upon period of manufacture.

SHATTUCK ARMS COMPANY Hatfield, Mass.

.22 RF. 4-shot; D.A.; bottom frame extension is squeezed into frame to rotate firing pin and serves as trigger; 4

barrels, top 2 parallel and bottom 2 parallel; barrel group breaks from top down to load, "Unique" Vest Pocket Pistol.

.30 RF. 4-shot; D.A.; (same as above).

.32 RF. 4-shot; D.A.; (same as above).

Note: The "Unique" was patented by O. F. Mossberg, December 4, 1906, while in the employ of the J. Stevens Arms & Tool Company. In 1909, Mossberg sold his patent rights to this pistol to C. S. Shattuck for whom he had been an employee from 1897 to 1902. These palm pistols were made by Shattuck from 1909 to about 1915.

STARR ARMS COMPANY New York, N.Y.

.41 RF. 4-shot; S.A.; button trigger; side hammer; barrel group breaks up from breech block on hinge at front of frame; brass frame; "Starr's Pats. May 10, 1864."

.32 RF. 4-shot; S.A.; (same as above).

WESSON, FRANKLIN Worcester, Mass.

.22 RF. 2-shot; S.A.; sp. tr.; 2 barrels superposed; barrels revolved manually to alternate position for firing; Patented December 15, 1868, "Vest Pocket" pistol.

Distinguishing feature: Hammer spur consists of small ring.

.22 RF. 2-shot; S.A.; sp. tr.; 2 barrels superposed; barrels revolved manually to alternate position for firing; regulation high hammer spur; Pat. December 15, 1868.

.32 RF. 2-shot; S.A.; sp. tr.; (same as above).

.41 RF. 2-shot; S.A.; sp. tr.; (same as above).

Note: The above double derringers are considerably larger and heavier than the "Vest Pocket" model.

.41 RF. 2-shot; S.A.; sp. tr.; 2 barrels superposed.

.32 RF. 2-shot; S.A.; sp. tr.; 2 barrels superposed.

Note: Double derringers in the above two calibers were produced with sliding dagger blade housed between the two barrels.

CHAPTER 6

Semi-Automatic Pistols

Colt's Patent Fire Arms Manufacturing Company introduced the first American semi-automatic pistol at the turn of the century (1900). It was the ingenious creation of an American inventor who was obliged to go to Europe to gain the reception he merited. John M. Browning is regarded in many circles as the greatest firearms inventor who ever lived and he certainly ranks foremost among designers of automatic weapons.

The Colt officials were the first American firearms manufacturers to recognize Browning's genius and make arrangements to utilize his patents on semi-automatic pistols. Colt semi-automatic pistols have been basically Browning designs. The Colt Model 1911 (a later modification designated 1911-A1) semi-automatic pistol has been the standard United States military sidearm for the past half century.

While the semi-automatic pistol has been available since the dawn of the twentieth century, it has never found the great favor in America such as has been accorded the revolver with the exception of .22 caliber target models. Other than the military Colt .45, semi-automatics in calibers larger than .22 have been primarily made and sold as personal protection arms. Recently, however, accurized target versions of the .45 ACP and .38 Special have come into prominence in competitive shooting and are being produced commercially. Thus the number of American manufacturers of semi-automatic pistols is not large and the range of models is relatively small in comparison with revolvers.

COLT'S PATENT FIRE ARMS MANUFACTURING CO. Hartford, Conn.

Model 1900 Sporting. .38 ACP; 7-shot mag.; 6-inch barrel; spur-type hammer; no slide stop; only safety was a movable rear sight which pressed down to block hammer from firing pin; Browning's Pat. April 20, 1897. Discontinued 1902.

Model 1902 Sporting. .38 ACP; 7-shot mag.; 6-inch barrel; rounded hammer thumbpiece; slide stop left side; no safeties; Pat. September 9, 1902. Discontinued 1908.

Model 1902 Military. .38 ACP; 8-shot mag.; 6-inch barrel; rounded hammer thumbpiece changed to spur hammer in 1908; slide stop left side; no safeties; grip squared and longer than on Model 1902 Sporting; Pat. September 9, 1902. Discontinued 1928.

Model 1903 Pocket. .38 ACP; 7-shot mag.; 4½-inch barrel; rounded hammer thumbpiece changed to spur hammer in 1908; no slide lock; no safeties; lugs on barrel fit into corresponding receiver recesses; takedown effected by pressing in on toggle catch below muzzle and removing toggle. Pat. September 9, 1902. Discontinued 1927.

Pocket Model 32. .32 ACP; 8-shot mag.; 3¾-inch barrel; hammerless (concealed hammer); slide stop and thumb-operated slide lock safety on left side of frame; squeezer grip safety; available in .380 caliber with 7-shot magazine from 1908 until discontinuance in 1945. Pat. December 22, 1903.

Note: Magazine disconnector safety feature added some years after introduction. Introduced in 1903.

Model 1905 Military. .45 ACP, 7-shot mag.; 5-inch barrel; rounded hammer thumbpiece; slide stop on left side; no safeties; hammer changed to spur type in 1908; dis-

continued in 1911. Pat. December 19, 1905.

Pocket Model 25. .25 ACP; 6-shot mag.; 2-inch barrel; hammerless; slide stop and thumb-operated slide lock safety on left side of frame; squeezer grip safety; magazine disconnector safety provided beginning with Serial No. 141,000; Pat. December 22, 1903, January 25, 1910. Introduced in 1908, discontinued in 1946.

Note: This model is at times referred to as "Colt's Vest Pocket Auto."

Model 1911 Military or **Government Model.** .45 ACP; 7-shot mag.; 5-inch barrel; spur type hammer; slide stop and thumb-operated slide lock safety on left side of frame; squeezer grip safety; Pat. February 14, 1911, August 19, 1913.

Note: This model and a later modification (Model 1911 A1) has been the official sidearm of the U.S. military forces for over half a century and may well be the most famous semi-automatic pistol ever designed as claimed by the Colt organization.

Target Model 22 (Woodsman). .22 RF L.R.; 10-shot mag.; 6½-inch barrel; adjustable front and rear sights; introduced in 1915 as the Target Model 22, designated "Woodsman" in 1927. Slide stop and slide lock safety left side of frame.

Match Target Woodsman. .22 RF L.R.; 10-shot mag.; 6½-inch barrel; fixed front sight with rear sight adjustable for both elevation and windage; 7 ounces heavier than the original Target Model 22; one-piece elongated walnut checkered grip; introduced in 1938 and still produced although in considerably modified styling.

Figure 11. SEMI-AUTOMATIC PISTOLS.
1. Colt Target (pre-Woodsman) .22. 2. Colt Pocket .380. 3. Colt Pocket .25. 4. Colt Model 1911 Government .45. 5. Warner Arms "Infallible" .32. 6. Smith & Wesson Model 41 .22.

Distinguishing feature: The original Match Target Woodsman has target rings and the words "Match Target" stamped on the barrel in front of the trigger guard. It should also have the one-piece grip although standard Woodsman grips were adaptable to this model.

Super 38. .38 Super ACP, 9-shot mag.; 5-inch barrel; fixed sights; same frame as Government Model 45; introduced in 1929 and still in current production.

Note: A Super Match 38 version was produced for a time but has been dropped. It incorporated a selected match barrel and the Stevens adjustable rear target sight.

Ace Target 22. .22 RF L.R.; 10-shot mag.; 4¾-inch barrel; target sights; same frame and safety features as Government Model 45; introduced in 1931, discontinued in 1941.

Ace Service Model 22. .22 RF L.R.; 10-shot mag.; 5-inch barrel; adjustable sights.

Note: This differed from the Ace Target Model 22 in that it incorporated a floating chamber which increased the recoil of .22 cartridges four times and simulated the recoil of the Government Model 45. The purpose of this feature was to provide practice analogous to firing the .45 ACP model at a considerably lower cost for ammunition expended. Introduced in 1937, discontinued in 1941.

National Match 45. .45 ACP; 7-shot mag.; 5-inch barrel; target sights; introduced in 1933, discontinued in 1943.

Note: This is essentially an accurized and refined version of the Government Model 45.

Commander. .45 ACP, .38 Super, 9mm Luger; 7-shot mag. in .45, 9-shot mag. in .38 Super and 9mm Luger; 4¼-inch barrel; fixed sights; round hollow-ring hammer spur. Introduced in 1951; still current.

Note: This is a lightweight version of the Government

Model 45 and Super 38 with the additional choice of the 9mm Luger caliber.

Gold Cup National Match 45. .45 ACP, 5-shot mag.; 5-inch barrel; target sights; essentially a revival of the former National Match 45. Introduced in 1957.

Gold Cup National Match 38. .38 Spl. mid-range, or wad cutter; 5-shot mag.; 5-inch barrel; target sights; second in Gold Cup series. Introduced in 1961.

Woodsman Sport Model 22.*
Targetsman 22.*
Huntsman 22.*
Junior Colt.

Note: See chapter 8 covering models above asterisked. The Junior Colt is made in Spain by Astra and will therefore be ignored in this book on American cartridge handguns.

GRANT HAMMOND MANUFACTURING CORPORATION New Haven, Conn.

.45 ACP. 8-shot mag.; 6¾-inch barrel; Patented May 4, 1915.

Distinguishing feature: Magazine ejects automatically when empty.

Note: One reference states that only eleven specimens of this model were made for U.S. Government tests. It was apparently never produced for the commercial market.

HARRINGTON & RICHARDSON ARMS COMPANY Worcester, Mass.

Self-Loading 32. .32 ACP, 8-shot mag.; 3½-inch barrel; hammerless (internal spring-compressed striker); no slide stop; thumb-operated safety left side of frame; squeezer grip safety; trigger guard of spring steel with lug for locking barrel via undercut; slide removed forward when barrel is released; patented August 20, 1907, April 13, 1909, and November 9, 1909.

Self-Loading 25. .25 ACP; 6-shot mag.; 2-inch barrel; hammerless; no slide stop; thumb-operated safety left side of frame; trigger guard of spring steel with lug for locking barrel via undercut; slide removed forward when barrel is released; patented August 20, 1907, and April 13, 1909.

HARTFORD ARMS & EQUIPMENT COMPANY Hartford, Conn.

.22 RF. 10-shot mag.; 6¾-inch barrel; frame design and appearance similar to earliest High Standard semi-automatics. Made in both .22 Short and .22 L.R. models.

Note: This model was produced in limited quantity during the late 1920's and early 1930's. Machinery and manufacturing rights of this firm were absorbed by the High Standard Manufacturing Company in 1932.

HIGH STANDARD MANUFACTURING CORPORATION Hamden, Conn.

Model B. .22 RF L.R.; 10-shot magazine, 4½-inch or 6¾-inch barrel; slide and sear lock thumb-safety latch left side of frame; hammerless (concealed hammer); fixed sights. The earliest model had takedown latch for removing slide on the left side of the frame immediately to the rear of the safety latch; a later issue of this model had the takedown latch on the right side of the frame. The plunger on the top of the slide just forward of the rear sight must be held down during takedown operation. Weight with long barrel, 33 ounces.

Note: The Model B semi-automatic pistol was High Standard's first entry in the handgun field and was introduced in 1932 some time after High Standard acquired the defunct Hartford Arms & Equipment Company. Discontinued 1944.

Figure 12. SEMI-AUTOMATIC PISTOLS.
1. Harrington & Richardson Self-Loading .32. 2. Harrington & Richardson Self-Loading .25. 3. Remington Model 51 .32. 4. Ruger Standard .22. 5. Savage Model 1907 .32. 6. Savage Model 1917 .32.

Model C. .22 RF Short; identical to the Model B with the exception of being chambered for .22 Short only and having a special magazine to handle the .22 Short cartridges; available with 6¾-inch barrel only; manufactured first with takedown latch on left side of frame, later installed on right side of frame. Discontinued 1942.

Model S-B. .22 RF L.R. Shot. Identical to the Model B with the exception of being chambered for .22 L.R. Shot cartridges only; barrel bored smooth with no choke. Available with 6¾-inch barrel only. Discontinued 1941.

Note: During a visit at the High Standard Factory in the summer of 1961, the author was informed by officials that less than 100 of this model were produced as they were not considered successful. It may be redundant to point out that this model would constitute a rare find for collectors.

Model A. .22 RF L.R.; 10-shot magazine; 4½-inch or 6¾-inch barrel; same weight barrel as the Model B; longer handle and grips than the Model B; slide locks open automatically after last shot is fired; target sights. Manufactured first with takedown latch on left side of frame, later installed on right side of frame. Weight with long barrel, 36 ounces. Discontinued 1942.

Model D. .22 RF L.R.; 10-shot magazine; 4½-inch or 6¾-inch barrel; barrel weight 4 ounces heavier than on Models B and A; long handle and grips as in Model A; automatic slide lock; target sights. Manufactured first with takedown latch on left side of frame, later installed on right side of frame. Weight with long barrel, 40 ounces. Discontinued 1942.

Model E. .22 RF L.R.; 10-shot magazine; 4½-inch or 6¾-inch barrel; barrel weight 6 ounces heavier than on Models B and A; barrel, slide and frame perfected and aligned along the entire top of the pistol; long handle and grips as in Model A; automatic slide lock; target sights;

target grips with thumb rest standard; manufactured first with takedown latch on left side of frame, later installed on right side of frame. Weight with long barrel, 42 ounces. Discontinued 1942.

Note: In 1939 High Standard brought out a line of exposed hammer semi-automatic pistols: H-B, H-A, H-D, and H-E. Inasmuch as these were basically the same as the hammerless models of the same designation, only the differentiating features will be cited. The safety on Models H-B, H-A, H-D, and H-E was the disconnection of the sear bar when the hammer was drawn back to the half-cock position. The H-B model was produced for a time after World War II with a slide and sear lock thumb-latch safety on the left side of the frame. The takedown latch on the hammer models was invariably on the right side of the frame.

Model H-D Military. .22 RF L.R.; 10-shot magazine; 4½-inch and 6¾-inch barrel; exposed hammer; slide and sear lock thumb-safety latch on left side of frame; target sights; takedown latch on right side of frame. Weight with long barrel, 41 ounces.

Note: This model was produced in considerable volume from 1943 to 1950. It was employed extensively by the United States armed forces for training purposes and by civilian competitive shooters in the early years following W.W. II.

Model G-.380. .380 ACP; 6-shot magazine; 5-inch barrel; exposed hammer; slide and sear lock thumb-safety latch on left side of frame; fixed sights; detachable barrel; weight 40 ounces.

Note: This is the first of High Standard's G series models which featured removable and interchangeable barrels. The barrel is free to move forward and off of frame when the lug of a spring-actuated catch forward of the trigger guard is released by thumb pressure. The slide is also removed forward following removal of barrel. The lug of barrel catch fits with precision and pressure into undercut of barrel base lug for positive locking. The G-.380 was reputedly designed for the United States O.S.S. in 1943 and was produced commercially from 1947 to 1950. The Model G-.380 remains the only semi-automatic pistol produced by High Standard to date (1962) in a caliber other than .22 RF.

Model G-B. .22 RF L.R.; 10-shot magazine; 4½-inch and 6¾-inch barrel; hammerless (concealed hammer); slide and sear lock thumb-safety latch on left side of frame; fixed sights. Weight with long barrel, 36 ounces. No automatic slide lock following final shot.

Model G-D. .22 RF L.R.; 10-shot magazine; 4½-inch and 6¾-inch barrel; hammerless (concealed hammer); slide and sear lock thumb-safety latch on left side of frame; target sights; heavier barrel and longer handle frame than Model G-B; automatic slide lock. Weight with long barrel, 41 ounces.

Model G-E. .22 RF L.R. Same general specifications as Model G-D with the exception of a heavier barrel which increased weight with long barrel to 44 ounces and the left grip was provided with a thumb rest as a standard feature.

Note: The G series in .22 caliber was introduced in 1949 and discontinued in 1952. All were constructed with the same takedown system as described under Model G-.380. All were hammerless (concealed hammer) and did not have a magazine disconnector safety.

Olympic. .22 RF Short; 10-shot magazine; original issue of this model was basically the Model G-E adapted for the .22 RF Short cartridge and initially was offered in 4½-inch barrel only. This first issue was introduced in 1949 and discontinued in 1950.

Olympic (Second Issue). .22 RF Short; 10-shot magazine; 4½-inch and 6¾-inch barrel; hammerless (concealed hammer); new type and smaller slide and sear lock thumb-safety left side of frame; target sights; barrels are ribbed underneath for mounting adjustable weights; automatic slide lock; weight with long barrel, 39 ounces; same takdown system as G series. Introduced in 1950.

Supermatic. .22 RF L.R.; 10-shot magazine; 4½-inch and 6¾-inch barrel; same general specifications as the Olympic (Second Issue) except chambered for .22 Long Rifle cartridges only; weight with long barrel, 42 ounces. Introduced in 1950.

Note: In 1954, the Olympic and Supermatic models had precision-aligned muzzle stabilizers built into the 6¾-inch barrels. The Olympic and Supermatic models underwent major modification in 1958.

Field King. .22 RF L.R.; same general specifications as the Supermatic except the barrel is not milled for mounting adjustable barrel weights or a different front sight. Introduced in 1950 and discontinued in 1958.

Sport King. .22 RF L.R.; 10-shot magazine; 4½-inch and 6¾-inch barrel; hammerless (concealed hammer); positive sear lock thumb-safety; solid steel stop lug; push-button takedown; fixed sights; weight with long barrel, 40 ounces. The all-steel model was introduced in 1952 and in 1956 this model was made available with choice of frame made from a lightweight high-tensile forged missile-alloy. Weight of this forged aluminum frame model is 30 ounces with the longer barrel.

Flite King. .22 RF Short; same general specifications as the Sport King model except chambered for .22 Short cartridges and with appropriate magazine to accommodate same. Introduced in 1954 in the lightweight version with frame and slide made of high-tensile forged missile-alloy

aluminum; an all-steel version was added later. Weight with long barrel, 26 ounces. The lightweight Flite King was discontinued in 1960.

Dura-Matic. .22 RF L.R.; 10-shot magazine; 4½-inch and 6½-inch barrel; hammerless (concealed hammer); positive cross-bolt safety; barrel is fastened to frame by a serrated nut just forward of the trigger guard, the nut having three slots which permits a coin to be used as a spanner for turning; push-button magazine release; weight with long barrel, 34 ounces. Introduced in 1954.

Note: In 1956 High Standard began the manufacture of the J. C. Higgins Model 80 semi-automatic pistol to be marketed exclusively through Sears, Roebuck & Company. Basically this is the Dura-Matic with modifications in contour. The barrel is flat-sided and it sports plastic grips featuring a large S-shaped thumb-rest with metal disk insert on the left side for engraving initials. This one-piece grip can be installed on the Dura-Matic only if the Model 80 trigger guard is also installed. The Model 80 has fixed sights and a visible indicator when cocked (red dot on end of firing pin protrudes through rear of slide) as does the Dura-Matic.

Supermatic Trophy.
Supermatic Citation.
Supermatic Tournament.
Olympic Citation.

Note: The above four .22 target semi-automatic pistols were introduced in 1958 and represent a radical redesigning of the former Supermatic and Olympic models. Specifications are covered fully in chapter 8.

Figure 13. SEMI-AUTOMATIC PISTOLS
1. High Standard Supermatic. 2. Reising "Bear." 3. Whitney. 4. High Standard Flite-King, Light Weight. 5. High Standard Model B. 6. High Standard Model G.—.380.

KIMBALL ARMS COMPANY Detroit, Mich.

.30 U.S. Carbine. 7-shot magazine; 3-inch and 5-inch barrel; hammerless; fixed barrel, slide removed to rear; "Combat" model had 3-inch barrel with fixed sights; "Target" model had 5-inch barrel with Micro rear target sight.

Note: The Kimball semi-automatic pistol was produced commercially in 1958. It was found by impartial tests to be of unsafe design for the powerful .30 U.S. carbine cartridge. Production of this pistol was discontinued prior to the granting of a U.S. patent.

PHOENIX ARMS COMPANY Lowell, Mass.

.25 ACP. 6-shot magazine; 2¼-inch barrel; approximately the size of the Colt .25 Pocket Model; retractor spring is in housing above the barrel; produced in limited volume during the second decade of this century.

Note: The author has been unable to verify the existence of a .32 ACP semi-automatic pistol reputedly manufactured by Phoenix.

REISING MANUFACTURING CORPORATION Hartford, Conn.

.22 RF L.R. 10-shot magazine; 6¾-inch barrel; exposed hammer; no manual safety but hammer has half-cock; magazine disconnector safety; barrel hinged to front of frame which extends beyond trigger guard; takedown (barrel release) button directly above trigger; mainspring in handle behind magazine well. Left brown rubber grip has an embossed picture of a bear's head and fore feet with the words "Reising" above and "It's A Bear" below; patented May 16, 1916, October 25, 1921. Produced from 1920 to 1928.

REMINGTON ARMS COMPANY, INC. Ilion, N.Y.

Model 51. .32 ACP; .380 ACP; 7-shot magazine; 3⅜-inch barrel; thumb-latch safety to rear left side of receiver; squeezer grip safety which remains in grip until cocked;

magazine disconnector safety; magazine release button just to rear of trigger; caliber marked on barrel at ejection port and on magazine; slide milled flat on top and matted; both grips marked "Remington UMC" within a circle at top; hammerless (concealed hammer); barrel and slide removed forward after releasing barrel holding pin; Pedersen Patents March 9, 1920, August 3, 1920, October 12, 1920, June 14, 1921; approximately 70,000 of both calibers combined were produced between introduction in 1918 and discontinuance in 1934. Serial numbers preceded by letters PA. (Experimental .45 ACP model tested and rejected by United States military forces.)

Note: Remington was licensed to manufacture the Government Model .45 ACP semi-automatic during World Wars I and II inasmuch as Colt's facilities were unequal to the demand.

STURM, RUGER & COMPANY, INC.* Southport, Conn.

Standard Model .22 RF L.R. 9-shot magazine; 4¾-inch and 6-inch barrel; hammerless (concealed hammer); thumb-latch safety left side of frame behind grip locks sear and bolt and also manually locks bolt in open position; no magazine disconnector safety; weight 36 ounces with short barrel, 38 ounces with long barrel. Introduced in 1949, this semi-automatic was the first product of Sturm, Ruger & Co.

Note: Several unique Ruger design and construction features differentiate this semi-automatic from the typical. The grip frame incorporates the safety plus all the firing mechanism and is separate from the receiver-barrel assembly. The receiver is round with the barrel, which tapers toward the muzzle; they are permanently assembled via 20 pitch screw threads. The "slide" is a cylindrical bolt which

---

* This firm is listed alphabetically under the letter "R" inasmuch as all their handguns are referred to as "Rugers"—Sturm having died in 1951.

slides within the tubular housing of the receiver. The bolt contains the firing pin, extractor, and serves as the breech-block. The rear sight is fixed and mounted on the receiver, thus remaining stationary during the firing sequence. The rear of the bolt has grooved lugs for manual cocking. The receiver-barrel assembly is locked to the frame via two lugs—one in the grip frame pointing forward into a recess in the receiver, the other in the removable backstrap. Music wire coil springs are employed exclusively. The external appearance and grip shape of the Ruger are analogous to the German Luger.

Mark I Target Model. .22 RF L.R.; 9-shot magazine; 6⅞-inch barrel; same general specifications as Standard Model with following exceptions: Longer barrel of heavier weight, Micro rear target sight with click adjustments for windage and elevation, Patridge style wider front sight, specially-tuned target trigger, weight 42 ounces; muzzle brake available as optional accessory.

SAVAGE ARMS COMPANY Utica, N.Y.

Model 1907. .32 ACP, 10-shot magazine; 3¾-inch barrel; exposed burr-type rounded cocking piece attached to striker; thumb latch safety on left side of frame rear of grip; Indian Head trade-mark embossed in center of hard rubber grips; patented November 21, 1905 but not introduced commercially until 1907. The Model 1907 in .32 caliber was discontinued in 1916. .380 ACP; 9-shot magazine; same general specifications as above, this caliber was introduced in 1913 and discontinued in 1915.

Model 1915. .32 ACP, .380 ACP; 10-shot magazine (.32), 9-shot magazine (.380); hammerless (concealed cocking piece and striker); thumb-latch safety plus squeezer grip safety; slide stop at right side of receiver; this model was introduced in 1915 and discontinued in 1917.

Model 1917. .32 ACP, .380 ACP; 10-shot magazine (.32),

9-shot magazine (.380); spur-type cocking piece attached to striker exposed at rear of slide; thumb-latch safety on left side of frame rear of grip; thumb-latch safety manually locks slide in open position; caliber marked on top of slide; serial numbers at front of frame forward of trigger guard; Indian Head trade-mark embossed at top of hard rubber grips; broader handle than Models 1907 and 1915 with angled backstrap; patented November 21, 1905. Introduced in 1917, discontinued about 1925.

Note: A model was also made in .45 ACP, 8-shot magazine; 5¼-inch barrel; exposed burr-type rounded cocking piece attached to striker; squeezer grip safety; lanyard ring in butt. There were 200 of these experimental military models in .45 ACP caliber delivered to a special U.S. Ordnance Board at Springfield Armory during 1907. While tests demonstrated the Savage .45 compared very favorably with the Colt .45, the fact that Colt was prepared to meet government demands for quantity and delivery whereas Savage was not, proved a deciding factor in favor of Colt. Savage never produced this model commercially.

A pocket-size .25 ACP was also made; no valid source of information on this model could be obtained but its existence has been verified.

SMITH & WESSON Springfield, Mass.

.35 S&W Auto. 7-shot magazine; 3½-inch barrel; hammerless (concealed hammer). This model has a squeezer grip safety mounted in handle at the front and directly below the trigger guard—it is operated by the second finger. A thumb-operated wheel-type safety is mounted in handle at rear and above center; rolling the milled wheel up following cocking locks the firing mechanism. There is no magazine disconnector safety. The trigger guard is hinged to frame at front and acts as barrel release; the barrel is hinged to the frame at the top rear and swings up when released. The "slide" is a bolt breechblock which is ribbed for manual cocking. It contains the firing pin and extractor. The bolt breechblock has a disconnector permitting manual loading without necessity of compressing recoil spring. Introduced in 1913, discontinued in 1921.

.32 ACP. 7-shot magazine; 3½-inch barrel; hammerless (concealed hammer); squeezer grip safety mounted in handle at front as in .35 S&W model; magazine disconnector safety; barrel fixed to receiver inside two-part slide, rear portion of which is the bolt breechblock and can be retracted independently by releasing bolt disconnector located just above left grip as in .35 S&W model. Both sights are milled integral with the slide which encloses the entire top of the pistol. Introduced in 1924, discontinued in 1937.

Note: The above two pistols incorporated construction features patented by the manufacturers of the Clement .32 semi-automatic of Belgium. Smith & Wesson acquired these patent rights. Patent dates applicable to these two pistols are: September 13, 1910, December 13, 1910, February 28, 1911, July 30, 1912, and September 24, 1912. The .32 ACP model is avidly sought by collectors but is becoming difficult to locate with value soaring inordinately.

Model 39 DA. 9mm Luger; 8-shot magazine; 4-inch barrel; exposed spur-type hammer; thumb-latch safety left side of slide; magazine disconnector safety; automatic slide lock following final shot; frame and mainspring housing of lightweight alloy; revolver-type trigger both cocks and releases sear by one pull; introduced commercially in 1954.

Model 44 SA. 9mm Luger; 8-shot magazine; 4-inch barrel; same general specifications as Model 39 except trigger and action which is single as in majority of semi-automatics; introduced in 1955 and discontinued in 1957.

Note: The Model 39 DA is the first American manufactured double action semi-automatic pistol and remains currently the only such pistol produced in America.

Model 41. .22 RF L.R., 10-shot magazine; 7⅜-inch and 5-inch barrels; introduced in 1957. For complete specifications, see chapter 8.

Model 46. .22 RF L.R., 10-shot magazine; 7-inch and 5-inch barrels; introduced in 1959. For complete specifications, see chapter 8.

UNION FIREARMS COMPANY Toledo, O.

Manufactured a semi-automatic revolver during the first decade of this century. It was engineered to utilize recoil of detonated cartridge to turn cylinder to next chamber as well as cock hammer for next shot.

WARNER ARMS CORPORATION Norwich, Conn.
(DAVIS-WARNER ARMS CORP. 1917-1919 Assonet, Mass.)

.32 ACP. Hammerless, coiled spring-operated striker; "slide" is internal blow-back bolt; fixed barrel; thumb-safety latch just behind trigger guard left side of frame; patented by Warner July 28, 1914; March 9, 1915; "Infallible."

Note: The "Infallible" is found with various modifications and marked either "Warner Arms Corp." or "Davis-Warner Arms Corp."

WHITNEY FIREARMS, INC. North Haven, Conn.

.22 RF L.R. 10-shot magazine; 4⅝-inch barrel; exposed hammer partially shrouded by cocking piece at rear of bolt breechblock; one-piece frame with integral trigger guard houses barrel, magazine, and sliding bolt breechblock containing firing pin, extractor and cocking piece. Frame-trigger guard unit made of aluminum alloy; thumb-latch safety behind left grip rear of frame; magazine dis-connector safety; hammer has half-cock which prevents accidental discharge via dropping or otherwise bumping hammer but this is not the usual half-cock safety as it can be released by pulling the trigger; fixed sights, with top of frame flat and matted for glare-proof sighting; weight 23 ounces. Designed by Robert L. Hillberg, commercial production began in 1955. Some specimens marked "Wolverine."

CHAPTER 7

Sources For Handgun Collectors

Assuming the foregoing chapters have created, or further stimulated, the reader's interest or desire to become a collector of American cartridge handguns, how does one go about getting started in this fascinating hobby? What sources are available to you for obtaining specimens for your collection?

It is well-nigh imperative that anyone engaging in this activity seriously become an active member of a gun collectors association or, better yet, associations. Such associations have literally mushroomed since World War II.

Every gun collectors association stages from one to perhaps as many as six "gun shows" annually. Each show is usually of two days duration held on Saturdays and Sundays. At these "gun shows" collectors and gun dealers rent tables from the sponsoring association for the display of their wares with buying, selling, and "horse trading" ensuing for the duration of the meeting.

The Ohio Gun Collectors Association, of which the author is a Director and Historian, has the distinction of being the largest such association in the world. The O.G.C.A. is comprised of a membership in excess of 2,000 representing 38 states, the District of Columbia, and Canada. The year 1962 marked the Silver Anniversary of the O.G.C.A., it having begun quite informally in August, 1937, when some thirty or so men gathered by invitation at the residence of Miller Bedford, New London, Ohio. The spectacular growth of the Ohio Gun Collectors Association gave impetus to the formation of numerous other state associations and it is recognized as the "Father" of the state gun collector association movement now so widespread.

Three of the O.G.C.A.'s five annual "gun shows" are staged at the Veterans Memorial Exhibition Hall, Columbus, Ohio. Here some 550 tables of firearms, and firearm accessories, are on display. Each table being six foot, this figures out to 3,300 linear feet of exhibits! This will give the reader some idea of the vast selection offered by such an organization to its members who are seeking some particular specimen, or specimens, for their collection, and how the gathering of any type collection can be greatly facilitated by membership in such an association.

Ordinarily, the larger the gun show the greater will be the potential selection for the collector. However, the author has acquired some of his most prized and valuable pieces at the smaller local area gun shows which may run less than fifty tables of exhibits.

One might have the notion that he will see the same guns displayed, show after show, but this is not quite the case. Sometimes a person has to attend a number of consecutive shows before he spots the particular gun he has been seeking. Turnover of the more sought after items is high and sometimes a specific model will disappear from the shows for a spell but, if one is patient and persistent, it is bound to turn up again sooner or later.

There are out-and-out gun dealers who handle firearms for the basic purpose of making money. They may, or may not, possess a love for the commodities they deal in but generally anything they have in stock is for sale. Most dealers will take in other firearms in trade on their items but some refuse to do so. Collector items, of course, will only be found at dealers who trade in used, as well as new, guns. Gun dealers may maintain a retail store on a full-time basis or they may only operate at specified times such as evenings or weekends at their residence or an adjunct to their residence. Gun dealers, as noted earlier, who are members of gun collectors associations frequently set up shop at the various scheduled meetings, or "gun shows."

A few of the many dealers in general antiques also include firearms in their stock. One may have to hit quite a few such dealers, however, to ferret out those who handle guns and, even then, they may have but a small selection and the price may not be "right."

Another source not to be overlooked is that of the "retired" gun collector. We all know we can't take it (or them) with us and that one day we will either have to will our collection to our heirs or dispose of them ourselves. Thus there are collectors who for health, or other reasons, decide to give up the game and to let someone else enjoy the guns they have acquired and admired over the years. If you happen to hear about some collector who has arrived at this time of life, you may pick up some rare and fine pieces priced within reason and at no great effort. Widows of collectors who die or are killed unexpectedly seldom dispose of their husbands' collections themselves but consign them to another collector, or dealer, to sell.

To keep up with the collectors firearms market, it is advisable to subscribe to one or more publications specializing in this field. The newspaper-type publication which appears to have the biggest circulation catering exclusively to the firearms fraternity is *The Shotgun News*, published at Columbus, Nebraska. Its masthead proclaims it to be "The Trading Post for Anything That Shoots." It is issued twice a month and contains some 48 pages, tabloid-size, of advertisements of a display and classified nature. It takes considerable time and patience to wade through all the fine print but the chances are good that you will eventually spot what you have been looking for in some issue.

Most firearms magazines such as *The American Rifleman, Guns & Ammo* and *The Gun Report* have a classified advertisement section where individuals, or dealers, list from time to time desirable collectors items.

A word of caution seems appropriate here. The author would offer the counsel not to deal with anyone by letter or telephone who does not advertise, or give assurance of, return privileges in case of dissatisfaction or misrepresentation. The advertising media cannot vouch for the integrity of all of their clients and will not assume responsibility in their behalf.

One can follow up local newspaper classified ads placed by individuals and occasionally come up with a real buy or find but it has been the experience of the author that this is not too fruitful for the amount of time it can consume.

One can also place his own ad in local newspapers under the "Wanted to Buy" classification but, unless one is prepared to buy any gun that can be had at below market value, this can prove an inordinately time-consuming and nerve-racking (via answering the phone or door-bell) proposition to the collector of limited means and/or interests. It is not advocated for anyone other than a full-time dealer in firearms.

Another potential source for handgun collectors are the auctions which are held occasionally when firearms collections are to be disposed of in this manner. However, gun auctions are generally well-advertised and thus bring in dealers to bid against one another with the desirable items eventually reaching a figure, or bid, which renders those items a risky, or unsound, investment. Too, there is always the possibility that a "monied" individual will be present who will bid in the desirable item, or items, at a figure higher than its current valuation merely because he wants it and may have little concern as to what he could eventually realize on the piece should he decide to dispose of it.

As to auctions of miscellaneous merchandise, the time and travel expense involved in attending on the "long" chance that a valuable handgun will turn up amongst the household goods represents a poor investment unless one is retired, time has little value, and travel expense can be looked upon as "entertainment."

It may pay you to drop in at sporting goods, or hardware stores handling firearms in your vicinity or during your travels periodically to see what used or obsolete guns they may have taken in in trade on new, current firearms. The author has acquired a number of desirable items via this source and at prices below the "going rate" at collectors meetings.

The last source that will be reviewed is the Pawn Shop. The owner, or manager, of these shops is seldom expertly acquainted with firearms or informed as to their current values since he deals in so many commodities. The price he places on an unredeemed handgun may be considerably above, or (though less likely) significantly below, actual market value. In the former case you may not be able to convince him that an item you desire is grossly overpriced but in the latter case you may get yourself a genuine bargain. You must, of course, become quite knowledgeable yourself with respect to current values of used and obsolete handguns in order to recognize an economically sound as well as desirable investment.

The hoary economic principle of "Caveat Emptor" (let the buyer beware) applies to gun dealing as it does to most business transactions. Once a deal is consummated, it is most difficult, if not impossible, to obtain redress if the buyer later discovers he has been duped.

The topic of "faking" of parts, or whole handguns, has not been gone into inasmuch as this practice with respect to American cartridge handguns is virtually non-existent at this time. These handguns, with a few possible exceptions, have not yet attained high enough values on the collectors market to make the faking of them sufficiently profitable to unscrupulous operators in the firearms field.

CHAPTER 8

Current American
Cartridge Handguns
Illustrated

Buddie Arms—"DOUBLE DEUCE" DERRINGER

Caliber: .22 (Short, Long, and Long Rifle).
No. of Shots: 2—O/U.
Barrel Length: 2⅞ inches.
Weight: 12½ ounces.
Grips: White Franzite.
Finish: Blue, chrome, 24 karat gold.
Features: Adjustable coil mainspring; button rifling.

Colt—SINGLE ACTION ARMY

Caliber: .45 Colt, .38 Special, .44 Special, and .357 Magnum.

Ammunition: .45 Long Colt, .38 Special, .44 Special, and .357 Magnum.

No. of Shots: 6.

Barrel Length: 4¾ inches, 5½ inches, and 7½ inches in .45 Colt, .38 Special, and .357 Magnum. 5½ inches and 7½ inches in .44 Special.

Overall Length: 11½ inches with 5½-inch barrel, 13½ inches with 7½-inch barrel, and 10¾ inches with 4¾-inch barrel.

Weight: .45 cal. with 5½-inch barrel, 37 ounces; with 7½-inch barrel 39 ounces. .38 Special or .357 Magnum with 5½-inch barrel, 41 ounces; with 7½-inch barrel, 43 ounces.

Sights: Fixed.

Finish: Case hardened frame; blued barrel, cylinder, trigger guard and backstrap. Nickel optional. Smooth trigger, knurled hammer spur.

Grips: Checkered ebony rubber, square butt standard. Walnut grips available.

Colt—SINGLE ACTION FRONTIER SCOUT

Caliber: .22 Short, Long, Long Rifle or .22 Magnum Rimfire.
No. of Shots: 6.
Barrel Length: 4¾ inches.
Overall Length: 9⁵⁄₁₆ inches.
Weight: 24 ounces.
Sights: Fixed.
Finish: All blue or duotone. Smooth trigger, knurled hammer spur.
Grips: Checkered ebony composition. Walnut grips available.
Features: Same classic lines as Single Action Army.

Colt—BUNTLINE SPECIAL

Caliber: .45.

Ammunition: .45 Long Colt.

No. of Shots: 6.

Action: Single.

Barrel Length: 12 inches.

Overall Length: 18 inches.

Weight: 43 ounces.

Sights: Fixed.

Finish: Case hardened frame; blued barrel, cylinder, trigger guard, and backstrap. Trigger is smooth, hammer spur knurled.

Grips: Checkered ebony rubber. Smooth finish. Walnut grips available.

Colt—BUNTLINE SCOUT

Caliber: .22 Short, Long, Long Rifle or .22 Magnum Rimfire.

No. of Shots: 6.

Action: Single.

Barrel Length: 9½ inches.

Overall Length: 14¾ inches.

Weight: 28½ ounces.

Sights: Fixed.

Finish: All blue. Trigger is smooth, hammer spur knurled.

Grips: Standard checkered ebony composition. Walnut grips available.

Colt—PYTHON

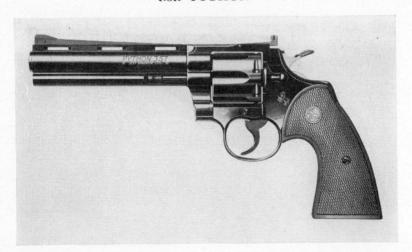

Caliber: .357 Magnum.

Ammunition: .357 Magnum; .38 Special (all types).

No. of Shots: 6.

Barrel Length: Either 4-inch or 6-inch barrels are available.

Overall Length: 9¼ inches or 11¼ inches depending on barrel.

Weight: With 4-inch barrel, 41 ounces; with 6-inch barrel, 44 ounces.

Sights: Adjustable rear sight; ramp front sight, ⅛-inch wide only.

Finish: Blue.

Grips: Full-checkered walnut, square butt, target type "gold" medallion.

Trigger: Grooved.

Features: Has wide, checkered hammer spur. Barrel has ventilated rib.

Colt—OFFICERS MODEL MATCH

Caliber: .38 Special, .22 Long Rifle, or .22 Magnum Rimfire.

Ammunition: .38 Special (mid-range, regular and high speed); .22 Long Rifle (regular and high speed). .22 Magnum Rimfire.

No. of Shots: 6.

Barrel Length: 6 inches.

Overall Length: 11¼ inches.

Weight: .38 cal., 39 ounces; .22 cal., 43 ounces.

Sights: Adjustable rear sight. ⅛-inch standard undercut front sight with removable blade. (¹⁄₁₀-inch by special order.)

Finish: Blue only.

Grips: Full checkered walnut, square butt, target type.

Trigger: Grooved.

Features: Hammer spur is wide and checkered.

Colt—TROOPER

Caliber: .38 Special, .22 Long Rifle, or .357 Magnum.

Ammunition: .38 Special (mid-range, regular and high speed); .22 Long Rifle (regular and high speed); .357 Magnum.

No. of Shots: 6.

Barrel Length: 4 inches.

Overall Length: 9¼ inches.

Weight: .38 cal., 34 ounces; .22 cal., 37 ounces.

Sights: Adjustable rear sight. Quick-draw ramp front sight, ⅛-inch wide.

Finish: Blue only. Trigger is grooved.

Grips: Full-checkered walnut, square butt.

Colt—OFFICIAL POLICE

Caliber: .38 Special or .22 Long Rifle.

No. of Shots: 6.

Barrel Length: .38 cal. in 4-inch, 5-inch, or 6-inch lengths. .22 cal. in 4- or 6-inch barrel.

Overall Length: 9¼ inches with 4-inch barrel, 10¼ inches with 5-inch barrel, 11¼ inches with 6-inch barrel.

Weight: .38 cal. with 6-inch barrel, 35 ounces; .22 cal. with 6-inch barrel, 38 ounces.

Sights: Fixed, ramp-style, glare-proofed.

Finish: Blue or nickel.

Grips: Checkered walnut, square butt. Round butt grips are optional on special order.

Trigger: Grooved.

Colt—POLICE POSITIVE SPECIAL

Caliber: .38 Special or .32 New Police.

Ammunition: .38 Special (mid-range and regular), .38 New Police, .38 S&W, .32 New Police, .32 S&W Short or Long.

No. of Shots: 6.

Barrel Length: 4 or 5 inches.

Overall Length: 8¾ inches with 4-inch barrel, 9¾ inches with 5-inch barrel.

Weight: .38 caliber, 23 ounces.

Sights: Fixed-type ramp-style, glare-proofed.

Finish: Blue or nickel.

Grips: Full-checkered walnut, round butt.

Features: A hammer shroud is available as an optional accessory.

Colt—AGENT

Caliber: .38 Special (mid-range and regular service loads).

No. of Shots: 6.

Barrel Length: 2 inches.

Overall Length: 6¾ inches.

Weight: 14 ounces. Lightweight alloy frame.

Sights: Fixed. Ramp-style, glare-proofed. Front blade .110 inch with rear notch .135 inch.

Finish: Blue only.

Grips: Checkered walnut, round butt.

Trigger: Grooved.

Features: A hammer shroud is available as an optional accessory.

Caliber: .38 Special or .32 New Police.

Ammunition: .38 Special (mid-range and regular), .38 New Police, .38 S&W, .32 New Police, .32 S&W Short & Long.

Barrel Length: .38 Special: 2 inches, 4 inches, or 5 inches. .32 New Police: 2 inches, 3 inches, or 4 inches.

Overall Length: 6¾ inches with 2-inch barrel, 7¾ inches with 3-inch barrel, 8¾ inches with 4-inch barrel, and 9¾ inches with 5-inch barrel.

Weight: 15 ounces. Lightweight alloy frame.

Sights: Fixed. Ramp-style, glare-proofed.

Finish: Blue only.

Grips: Full-checkered walnut, round butt.

Features: A hammer shroud is available as an optional accessory.

Colt—DETECTIVE SPECIAL

Caliber: .38 Special or .32 New Police.

Ammunition: .38 Special (mid-range, regular and high speed), .38 New Police, .38 S&W; .32 New Police and .32 S&W Short and Long.

Barrel Length: 2 inches.

Overall Length: 6¾ inches.

Weight: 21 ounces. All-steel construction.

Sights: Fixed. Ramp-style, glare-proofed.

Finish: Blue or nickel.

Grips: Checkered walnut, round butt.

Trigger: Grooved.

Features: A hammer shroud is available as an optional accessory.

Colt—WOODSMAN MATCH TARGET

Caliber: .22 Long Rifle.

No. of Shots: Magazine holds 10 rounds.

Action: Semi-automatic.

Barrel Length: Either 4½ or 6 inches.

Overall Length: 9 inches with 4½-inch barrel, 10½ inches with 6-inch barrel.

Weight: 40 ounces with long barrel, 36 ounces with 4½-inch barrel.

Sights: Adjustable rear sight. Ramp front sight with removable undercut blade.

Finish: Blue only.

Grips: Walnut with thumb rest.

Trigger: Wide.

Features: Slide stop is automatic. Weighted barrel is rectangular shape.

Colt—WOODSMAN TARGET MODEL

Caliber: .22 Long Rifle.

No. of Shots: Magazine holds 10 rounds.

Action: Semi-automatic.

Barrel Length: 6 inches.

Overall Length: 10½ inches.

Weight: 32 ounces.

Sights: Adjustable rear sight. Ramp front sight with removable blade.

Finish: Blue only.

Grips: Walnut with thumb rest.

Trigger: Wide.

Features: Slide stop is automatic.

Caliber: .22 Long Rifle.
No. of Shots: Magazine holds 10 rounds.
Action: Semi-automatic.
Barrel Length: 6 inches.
Overall Length: 10½ inches.
Weight: 31½ ounces.
Sights: Adjustable rear sight.
Finish: Blue only.
Grips: Walnut with thumb rest.
Trigger: Wide.
Features: This model does not have automatic slide stop.

Colt—WOODSMAN SPORT MODEL

Caliber: .22 Long Rifle.

No. of Shots: Magazine holds 10 rounds.

Action: Semi-automatic.

Barrel Length: 4½ inches.

Overall Length: 9 inches.

Weight: 30 ounces.

Sights: Adjustable rear sight. Ramp front sight with removable blade.

Finish: Blue only.

Grips: Walnut with thumb rest.

Trigger: Wide.

Features: Has automatic slide stop.

Colt—HUNTSMAN

Caliber: .22 Long Rifle.

Action: Semi-automatic.

Barrel Length: 4½ inches or 6 inches.

Overall Length: 9 inches with 4½-inch barrel; 10½ inches with 6-inch barrel.

Weight: Either 31½ ounces or 30 ounces depending on barrel length.

Sights: Fixed.

Finish: Blue only.

Grips: Walnut.

Trigger: Wide.

Features: No automatic slide stop

Colt—GOVERNMENT MODEL .45

Caliber: .45 Automatic.

No. of Shots: Magazine holds 7 rounds.

Action: Semi-automatic.

Barrel Length: 5 inches.

Overall Length: 8½ inches.

Weight: 39 ounces.

Sights: Fixed. Ramp, glare-proofed.

Finish: Blue or nickel.

Grips: Checkered Coltwood.

Safety: Features the standard Colt .45 grip and thumb safeties.

Trigger: Grooved.

Features: The hammer spur is checkered. Arched housing is featured.

Colt—COMMANDER

Caliber: .45 Automatic; .38 Super Automatic; 9mm Luger.

No. of Shots: .45 cal. magazines hold 7 rounds; the .38 and 9mm magazines hold 9 rounds.

Action: Semi-automatic.

Barrel Length: 4¼ inches.

Overall Length: 8 inches.

Weight: 26½ ounces.

Sights: Fixed, ramp-style, glare-proofed.

Finish: Blue only.

Grips: Checkered Coltwood.

Safety: This model has both the grip and thumb safeties.

Trigger: Grooved.

Features: Hammer spur is round-top and grooved. Housing is arched.

Colt—GOLD CUP NATIONAL MATCH

Caliber: .45.

Ammunition: .45 mid-range or .45 ACP.

No. of Shots: Magazine holds 5 rounds.

Action: Semi-automatic.

Barrel Length: 5 inches.

Overall Length: 8½ inches.

Weight: 37 ounces.

Sights: Front sight, vertical rear face. Improved adjustable rear sight.

Finish: Blue.

Grips: Walnut with gold-plated medallion.

Safety: Has the standard grip and thumb safeties.

Trigger: Standard housing is flat; arched housing is available. Hammer spur is serrated.

Colt—SUPER .38 AUTOMATIC

No. of Shots: Magazine holds 9 rounds.
Action: Semi-automatic.
Barrel Length: 5 inches.
Overall Length: 8½ inches.
Weight: 39 ounces.
Sights: Fixed, ramp-style, glare-proofed.
Finish: Blue or nickel.
Grips: Checkered Coltwood.
Safety: Standard Colt .45 grip and thumb safeties.
Trigger: Grooved.
Features: Hammer spur is grooved; housing is arched.

Colt—GOLD CUP NATIONAL MATCH, .38 SPECIAL

Ammunition: .38 Special, mid-range or wad cutter.
No. of Shots: 5.
Barrel Length: 5 inches.
Finish: Blue and matt finish.
Grips: Walnut.

Caliber: .22 RF Short.

Action: Single, with visible hammer; single shot.

Weight: 7¾ ounces.

Finish: Blue barrel, gold-plated frame and walnut grips or barrel and frame nickel-plated with imitation ivory grips.

Trigger: Spur-type.

Features: This is a replica of Colt's No. 3 Deringer of 1872 but in .22 rather than .41 caliber. Breech swings to right for loading and has automatic ejector.

Colt—CIVIL WAR CENTENNIAL

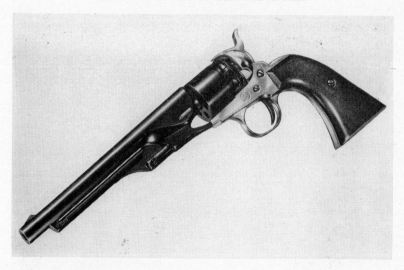

Caliber: .22 RF Short.
Action: Single action, single shot.
Finish: The barrel and dummy cylinder are finished in blue. Frame, trigger guard, and hammer are gold-plated.
Features: This model is a scaled-down replica of the 1860 Army model percussion Colt. It has a detachable barrel.

Great Western—SINGLE ACTION REVOLVER

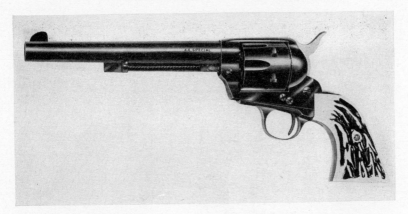

Caliber: Available in .22 RF, .22 Hornet, .357 Magnum, .38 Special, .44-40, .44 Special, .44 Magnum, .45 ACP, and .45 Long Colt.

No. of Shots: 6.

Barrel Length: 4¾ inches, 5½ inches, or 7½ inches.

Finish: Blue only.

Grips: Imitation stag.

Features: These are exact duplicates of the original Colt Single Action Army revolver except for incorporation of a floating firing pin in the frame.

Great Western—DERRINGER

Caliber: .38 S&W or .38 Special.

No. of Shots: 2.

Features: This is an over-under Double Derringer, externally an exact duplicate of the former Remington Double Derringer. It is single action, has spur trigger, and features coil springs and all-steel construction.

Harrington & Richardson—SPORTSMAN (Model 999)

Caliber: .22 (Short, Long, and Long Rifle).

No. of Shots: 9.

Action: Single and double action. Top-breaking and has automatic ejection.

Barrel Length: 6 inches.

Weight: 30 ounces.

Sights: Front with elevation adjustment; rear with windage adjustment.

Finish: Blue. Top surface of barrel has non-glare finish.

Grips: Checkered walnut, side grips with semi-thumb rest.

Features: This model has a target-weight barrel, wide hammer cocking spur, and coil springs are used throughout.

Harrington & Richardson—ULTRA "SIDEKICK"
(Model 939)

Caliber: .22 (Short, Long, and Long Rifle).

No. of Shots: 9.

Action: Single and double action. This model has a swing-out safety rim cylinder.

Barrel Length: 6 inches.

Weight: 33 ounces.

Sights: The rear sight is fully adjustable.

Finish: Blue.

Grips: Custom checkered walnut grips with full thumb rest.

Features: This model has a target-weight barrel with ventilated rib. Hammer has wide cocking spur. Exclusive safety lock and key.

Harrington & Richardson—SNAP-OUT
(Model 900)

Caliber: .22 (Short, Long, and Long Rifle).

No. of Shots: 9.

Action: Single and double action. Exclusive snap-out cylinder.

Barrel Length: 2½ inches, 4 inches, or 6 inches.

Weight: With 2½-inch barrel, 20 ounces; with 4-inch barrel, 25 ounces; with 6-inch barrel, 26 ounces.

Sights: Fixed.

Finish: Blue. A Model 901 is available in chrome.

Grips: Checkered white Tenite.

Safety: Automatic rebound hammer.

Features: This model has a snap-out cylinder-center pin unit for fast loading and unloading. All empties are extracted simultaneously by push pin. Construction features coil springs.

Harrington & Richardson—MODEL 622

Caliber: .22 (Short, Long, and Long Rifle).

No. of Shots: 6.

Action: Single and double action.

Barrel Length: 2½, 4, 6, and 10-inch barrels.

Weight: With 10-inch barrel, 32 ounces; 6-inch, 28 ounces; 4-inch, 26 ounces; 2½-inch barrel, 22 ounces.

Sights: Fixed.

Finish: Frame, velvet non-glare finish; other parts blue.

Grips: Checkered white Tenite.

Safety: Automatic rebound hammer.

Features: Square butt in contrast to the rounded butt of its companion chromed model (623). Completely enclosed cylinder pin release; simultaneous extraction of shells from removed cylinder accomplished by insertion of cylinder pin; coil mainspring.

Harrington & Richardson—"FORTY-NINER"
(Model 949)

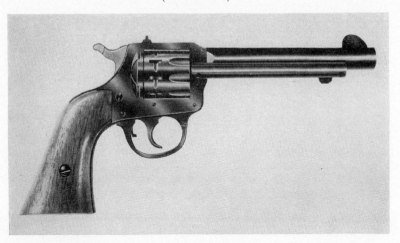

Caliber: .22 (Short, Long, and Long Rifle).
No. of Shots: 9.
Action: Single and double action.
Barrel Length: 5½ inches.
Weight: 31 ounces.
Sights: Adjustable rear sight. Western-style front blade.
Finish: Blue.
Grips: One piece Western-style, walnut.
Safety: Automatic rebound hammer.
Features: Loading gate is contoured. Unloading and extraction are accomplished by slide rod. This model has long wide hammer spur and heavyweight round barrel.

Harrington & Richardson—"SIDEKICK"
(Model 929)

Caliber: .22 (Short, Long, and Long Rifle).

No. of Shots: 9.

Action: Single and double action.

Barrel Length: 2½-inch, 4, 6, and 10-inch barrels.

Weight: With 2½-inch barrel, 22 ounces; 4-inch barrel, 26 ounces; 6-inch barrel, 28 ounces; 10-inch barrel, 32 ounces.

Sights: Wide blade front sight; windage adjustable rear sights on all versions except short barrel (2½-inch).

Finish: Blue with non-glare finish on top of frame. An all-chrome companion model in either 4- or 2½-inch barrel length is called "Sidekick, Model 930."

Grips: Checkered white Tenite.

Features: This model has a swing-out cylinder with automatic ejector return; swing-out cylinder employs a positive two-point locking system.

Harrington & Richardson—"GUARDSMAN"
(Model 732)

Caliber: .32 (chambered for .32 S&W and .32 S&W Long).

No. of Shots: 6.

Action: Single and double action.

Barrel Length: May be either 2½ or 4 inches.

Weight: 23½ ounces with short barrel; 26 ounces with 4-inch barrel.

Sights: Fixed blade front sight; the 4-inch barrel has windage adjustable rear.

Finish: Blue with non-glare finish on top of barrel and frame. An all-chromed version known as Model 733 is available in the short barrel length only.

Grips: Checkered white Tenite.

Safety: Automatic rebound hammer.

Features: The swing-out cylinder has automatic ejector return.

Harrington & Richardson—MODEL 970

Caliber: .22 Blank (RF).

Ammunition: Blank ammunition only.

No. of Shots: 9.

Action: Single and double action; center pin.

Barrel Length: Solid 2½-inch length.

Weight: 19 ounces.

Finish: Blue.

Grips: Checkered white Tenite.

Safety: Design prohibits use of cartridges other than blanks. Automatic hammer rebound safety is retained.

Features: Extraction is performed by push pin; all empties are ejected simultaneously. A Model 960 is the same except 6 shots, caliber .32.

Hi-Standard—DURA-MATIC

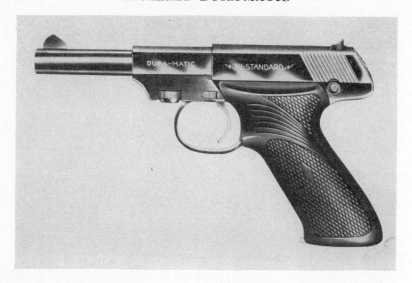

Caliber: .22 Long Rifle.
No. of Shots: 10.
Barrel Length: 4½- and 6½-inch barrels; interchangeable.
Sights: Square-notched rear.
Finish: Blue only.
Grips: Checkered plastic.
Safety: Cross-bolt type.
Trigger: Scored, non-slip.
Features: Barrel secured to frame by bolt and nut method.

Hi-Standard—SPORT-KING

Caliber: .22 Long Rifle.

No. of Shots: 10.

Barrel Length: 4½- and 6¾-inch barrels (one-piece) are interchangeable and designed for quick takedown.

Sights: Fixed.

Finish: Blue only.

Grips: Checkered plastic.

Safety: Double acting.

Trigger: Wide contour and serrated.

Features: This is the sporter version of the ISU OLYMPIC. It
features match-grade firing mechanism, jam-free ejection, and
has a chrome vanadium steel firing pin. Construction is all-steel.
A lightweight version of the SPORT-KING is available which
features a frame of forged missile-alloy. All other features identical with all-steel SPORT-KING.

Caliber: .22 Short.
No. of Shots: 10.
Barrel Length: 4½- and 6¾-inch lengths are available.
Finish: Blue only.
Grips: Checkered plastic.
Features: Same specification as all-steel **SPORT-KING** except
   chambered for .22 Short.

Hi-Standard—SUPERMATIC TOURNAMENT

Caliber: .22 Long Rifle.

No. of Shots: 10.

Barrel Length: 4½ and 6¾ inches.

Sights: Recoil-proof, wide square-notched rear sight with indexed positive click adjustment; undercut ramp front sight.

Finish: Blue only.

Grips: Checkered plastic.

Safety: Double acting.

Trigger: Wide target trigger; anti-backlash trigger-screw adjustment.

Hi-Standard—SUPERMATIC CITATION

Caliber: .22 Long Rifle.

No. of Shots: 10.

Barrel Length: 8-inch and 10-inch barrels; tapered.

Sights: Recoil-proof wide rear sight, square-notched with indexed click adjustments; undercut ramp front sight.

Grips: Checkered plastic.

Safety: Double acting.

Trigger: Adjustable pull with anti-backlash trigger-screw adjustment.

Features: Adjustable, removable barrel weights of 1.8 ounces and 2.6 ounces are optional. Firing pin is the rebounding type. Barrel stabilizer is detachable. Rear sight located forward of slide.

Hi-Standard—SUPERMATIC CITATION
(Tapered 6¾-inch barrel)

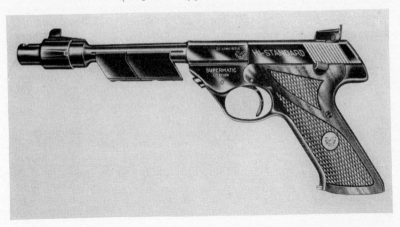

Features: This model preserves good sighting radius by locating the rear sight towards the rear of the slide—desirable with this shorter length barrel. All other features are identical with the 8- and 10-inch barrel versions of the Citation.

Hi-Standard—SUPERMATIC CITATION
(5½-inch Bull barrel)

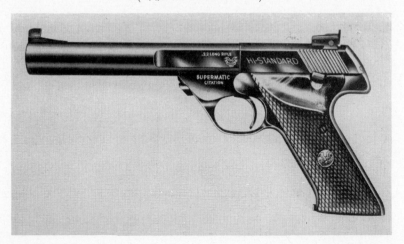

Features: The differences between this model and other Citations are chiefly in barrel length and configuration together with absence of a detachable barrel stabilizer, not needed with this version.

Hi-Standard—SUPERMATIC TROPHY

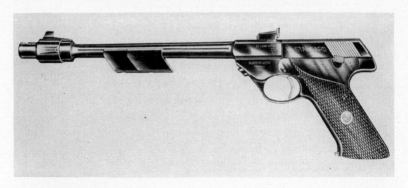

Caliber: .22 Long Rifle.

No. of Shots: 10.

Barrel Length: 8-inch and 10-inch barrels, tapered.

Weight: May be controlled with weights of 1.8 ounces and 2.6 ounces; these, of course, are detachable.

Sights: Recoil-proof wide rear sight, square notched with indexed click adjustments; undercut ramp front sight.

Finish: Has gold target-trigger, gold safety-button, and gold inlaid-lettering. Hand finished.

Grips: Checkered walnut.

Safety: Double acting.

Trigger: Pull adjustable; anti-backlash trigger-screw adjustment.

Features: Rear sight mounted forward of slide; detachable barrel stabilizer.

Hi-Standard—SUPERMATIC TROPHY
(6¾-inch barrel)

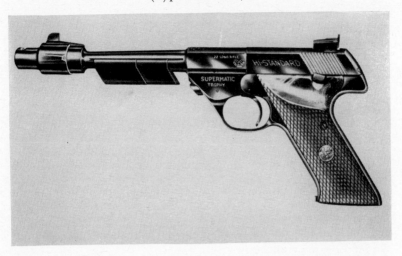

Features: Except that the rear sight is mounted on the slide, this model varies only in barrel length from the 8- and 10-inch barrel versions of the Trophy.

Hi-Standard—OLYMPIC

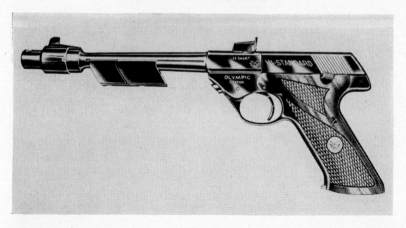

Caliber: .22 Short.

No. of Shots: 10.

Barrel Length: 8 inches.

Sights: Recoil-proof wide rear sight, square notched with indexed click adjustments; undercut ramp front sight.

Grips: Checkered plastic.

Trigger: Pull is adjustable; anti-backlash trigger-screw adjustment can be made.

Features: This model has a detachable barrel stabilizer; rear sight is mounted forward of slide.

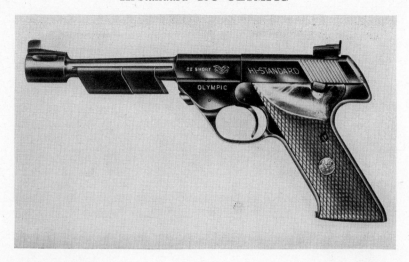

Caliber: .22 Short.
No. of Shots: 10.
Barrel Length: 6¾ inches. Integral stabilizer is cut into the barrel.
Grips: Checkered walnut.
Features: This pistol is made in two grades, one is called the
"Citation" grade, the other the "Trophy" grade. Features of the
Citation grade compare with the Supermatic Citation; the
Trophy grade compares mechanically with the Supermatic
Trophy. The ISU Olympic complies with all rapid fire pistol
regulations of the International Shooting Union. Rear sight is
mounted on slide at rear in this model.

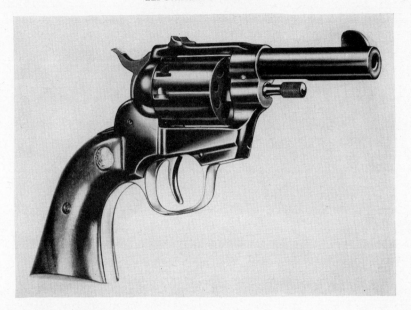

Caliber: .22 (Short, Long, and Long Rifle).
No. of Shots: 9.
Action: Double or single action.
Barrel Length: 3½ inches.
Weight: 23 ounces.
Sights: Fixed front; square-notched rear. Front blade is rounded to prevent catching in holster.
Finish: Barrel, blue finish; brass-finished backstrap and guard.
Grips: Walnut.
Features: Ejector is spring-loaded. This model is one of a High Standard series of Western-style replicas.

Hi-Standard—NATCHEZ

Barrel Length: 4½ inches.

Weight: 26 ounces.

Grips: Ivory composition, bird-head design.

Features: One of the High Standard series of Western replicas. Specifications except as indicated above are similar to the Posse model. The NATCHEZ features a dummy slide rod and housing.

Hi-Standard—DOUBLE—9

Caliber: .22 (Short, Long, and Long Rifle).

No. of Shots: 9.

Action: Double or single action.

Barrel Length: 5½ inches.

Weight: 28 ounces.

Sights: Fixed; front blade rounded; rear square-notched.

Finish: Blue or nickel.

Grips: Ivory-tone on blue model, ebony-black on nickel model.

Features: Dummy slide-rod and housing. Ejector is spring-loaded.

Note: The "Double-9" served as the prototype for the "Longhorn" series which in 5½-inch barrel length differs only in finish and style of grips. (See next page.)

Hi-Standard—LONGHORN

No. of Shots: 9.

Action: Double or single.

Barrel Length: 4½ inches.

Weight: 27 ounces.

Grips: Pearl or Ivory-style.

Safety: Rebounding hammer with automatic safety-block.

Features: The three Longhorn models differ in barrel length, weight, and style of grips. All are .22 caliber and accept 9 cartridges, Long, Short, or Long Rifle. All models incorporate a dummy slide rod and housing.

Hi-Standard—LONGHORN

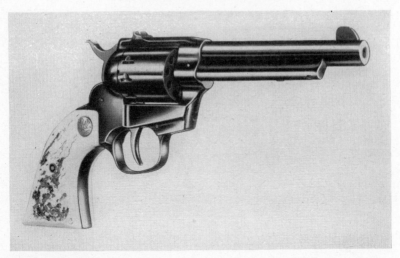

Barrel Length: 5½ inches.
Weight: 28 ounces.
Grips: Stag-style.

Hi-Standard—LONGHORN

Barrel Length: 9½ inches.
Weight: 32 ounces.
Grips: Walnut.
Features: The long barrel of this model is suggestive of a Buntline
replica—as intended.

Hi-Standard—SENTINEL SNUB

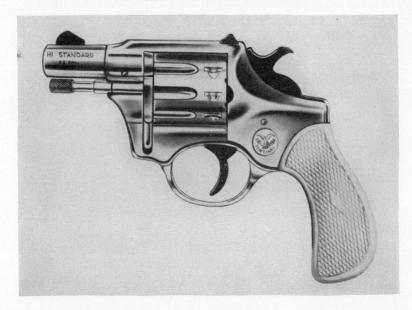

Caliber: .22 (Short, Long, and Long Rifle).

No. of Shots: 9.

Action: Single and double.

Barrel Length: 2⅜ inches.

Weight: 20 ounces.

Sights: Fixed ramp front sight; square-notched rear.

Finish: Blue or nickel.

Grips: Brown checkered grips on blued model; pearl-white checkered grips on nickel model. The grip of the Snub model is of bird-head design.

Safety: Rebounding hammer with automatic safety block.

Features: Barrel and cylinder are of high-tensile steel. Extraction of empty cases from cylinder results in ejection of all nine cases at once; the spring-loaded ejector then instantly returns to loading position.

Hi-Standard—SENTINEL (4 INCH)

Barrel Length: 4 inches.

Weight: 23 ounces.

Finish: Blue or nickel finish.

Grips: Checkered; brown on blued guns, pearl-white on nickel models; one-piece.

Features: Rigid frame of one-piece design, no screws. Other features such as caliber, action, etc., are those common to the Sentinel line.

Note: All SENTINEL models shown shoot nine .22 Shorts, Longs, or Long Rifles.

Hi-Standard—SENTINEL (6 INCH)

Barrel Length: 6 inches.
Weight: 24 ounces.
Finish: Blue or nickel.
Features: Same as the Sentinel in 4-inch barrel.

Hi-Standard—SENTINEL IMPERIAL (4 INCH)

Action: Double and single.
Barrel Length: 4 inches.
Weight: 22 ounces.
Sights: Serrated long-ramp front; wide, square-notched, movable rear.
Finish: Blue or nickel.
Grips: Two-piece walnut, diamond checkered.
Safety: Rebounding hammer with automatic safety block.
Trigger: Wide, target-grooved trigger.
Features: Frame is constructed of missile-alloy. Other features are those common to the Sentinel line.

Hi-Standard—SENTINEL IMPERIAL (6 INCH)

Barrel Length: 6 inches.
Weight: 25 ounces.
Finish: Blue or nickel.
Features: Same as the 4-inch barrel, Sentinel Imperial.

Hi-Standard—SENTINEL SNUB (COLORS)

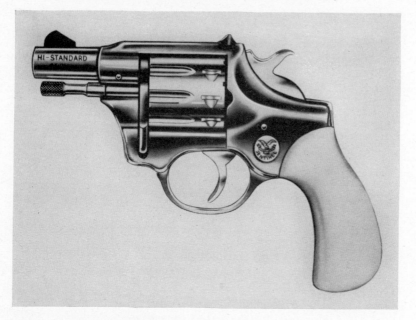

Barrel Length: 2⅜ inches.

Grips: Ivory-tone bird-head design, satin finished.

Features: Same specifications as regular SENTINEL SNUB with exception of finish; missile-alloy frame available in gold, turquoise, and pink.

Iver Johnson—MODEL 55-"TARGET"

Caliber: 22 (Short, Long, and Long Rifle).
No. of Shots: 8.
Action: Double and single.
Barrel Length: 4½-inch and 6-inch barrels.
Overall Length: 10¾ inches with 6-inch barrel.
Weight: 30½ ounces with 6-inch barrel.
Sights: Fixed.
Finish: Blue only.
Grips: Checkered plastic, with thumb-rest.
Features: Solid frame construction.

Iver Johnson—MODEL 55S-"CADET"

Caliber: .22.
Ammunition: .22 (Short, Long, and Long Rifle).
No. of Shots: 8.
Action: Double or single.
Barrel Length: 2½ inches.
Overall Length: 7 inches.
Weight: 24 ounces.
Sights: Fixed.
Finish: Blue only.
Grips: Semi-rounded butt; pocket-size.
Features: This model is a small, light, pocket or kit gun built on a solid frame.

Iver Johnson—MODEL 56-"STARTER"

Caliber: Blank cartridges only: .22 or .32.

No. of Shots: .22—8; .32—5.

Barrel Length: 2½ inches; solid.

Overall Length: 6¾ inches.

Weight: 10 ounces.

Finish: Blue only.

Grips: Tenite.

Features: This model is made for use at sporting events, in dog training, etc.

Iver Johnson—MODEL 57-"TARGET"

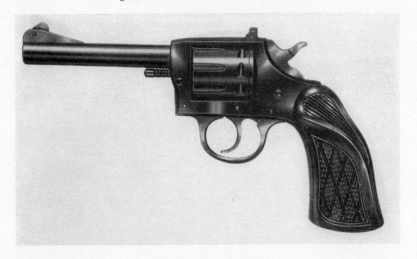

Caliber: .22 (Short, Long, and Long Rifle).

No. of Shots: 8.

Action: Double and single.

Barrel Lengths: Available in 2½-inch, 4½-inch, or 6-inch barrel lengths.

Overall Length: With 6-inch barrel, 10¾ inches.

Weight: 30½ ounces with 6-inch barrel.

Sights: Adjustable, both front and rear.

Grips: Checkered plastic, with thumb-rest.

Features: Solid frame construction; target sights.

Iver Johnson—TRAILSMAN
(Model 66)

Caliber: .22 (Short, Long, and Long Rifle).

No. of Shots: 8.

Action: Double and single.

Barrel Length: 4½ or 6 inches.

Overall Length: With longer barrel, 11 inches; shorter barrel, 9½ inches.

Weight: 31 or 34 ounces, depending on barrel.

Sights: Front adjustable for elevation, rear for windage.

Finish: Blue only.

Grips: Checkered plastic, with thumb rest.

Features: Barrel is chrome lined. Top-break construction with rear sight mounted on barrel catch; thumb-ejector under barrel; target sights.

Iver Johnson—SNUB MODEL 66

Caliber: .22, .32 S&W, or .38 S&W.

Ammunition: .22 handles Short, Long, and Long Rifle. Colt New Police ammunition may be used in either the .32 or .38, as well as regulation .32 or .38 S&W.

No. of Shots: .22—8; 5-shot in other calibers.

Action: All Iver Johnson revolvers may be fired single or double action.

Barrel Length: 2¾ inches.

Overall Length: 7 inches.

Weight: 25 ounces.

Sights: Front fixed; rear adjustable for windage.

Finish: Blue only.

Grips: Rounded butt; Tenite, pocket size.

Features: Chrome lined barrel. Same construction and ejection features as regular TRAILSMAN.

Iver Johnson—SIDEWINDER
(Model 50)

Caliber: .22 (Short, Long, and Long Rifle).
No. of Shots: 8.
Action: Double and single.
Barrel Length: 6 inches.
Overall Length: 11¼ inches.
Weight: 31 ounces.
Sights: Fixed.
Grips: American walnut.
Safety: Half-cock.
Features: This is a Western-style revolver with solid frame, loading
  gate, slide rod ejector, and wide hammer spur.

Ruger—STANDARD MODEL

Caliber: .22 Long Rifle only.

No. of Shots: 9-shot magazine.

Barrel Length: 4¾ or 6-inch barrels.

Overall Length: 8¾ inches or 10 inches depending on barrel length.

Weight: 36 ounces in shorter barrel version; 38 ounces with 6-inch barrel.

Sights: Fixed.

Grips: Hard rubber.

Safety: Locks sear and bolt; cannot be put in safe position unless gun is cocked.

Trigger: Grooved, curved finger surface, ⅜-inch wide. Has two-stage pull.

Features: Barrel has 6 groove rifling; twist one in 14 inches. Music wire springs are used throughout. Magazine is detachable.

Ruger—MARK I TARGET MODEL

Caliber: .22 Long Rifle only.

No. of Shots: 9-shot magazine.

Barrel Length: 6⅞ inches, heavyweight, burnish reamed.

Overall Length: 10⅞ inches.

Weight: 42 ounces.

Sights: Patridge style, front blade, .125 inches wide, undercut to prevent glare. Micrometer rear sight, click adjustments for windage and elevation. Sight radius, 9⅜ inches.

Trigger: Pull designed for target shooting.

Features: A muzzle brake is optional in this model. Other specifications are similar to the Standard model.

Ruger—SINGLE-SIX

Caliber: .22 or .22 W.M.R.

Ammunition: Conventional .22 Short, Long, and Long Rifle or in .22 W.M.R. caliber, will accept the new .22 Winchester Magnum Rimfire.

No. of Shots: 6.

Action: Single.

Barrel Length: Barrels of 4⅝, 5½, 6½, and 9½ inches are made.

Sights: Fixed, wide blade, Patridge style front; square-notched rear. Rear sight is mounted in dovetail in flat top frame.

Finish: Blued.

Grips: Walnut.

Features: Independent alloy steel firing pin mounted in frame. Recessed chambers. Construction features chrome molybdenum steel and music wire springs.

An extra fitted cylinder is an optional accessory with the Single-Six convertible model thus permitting use in either of the calibers listed.

Ruger—BEARCAT

Caliber: .22 (Short, Long, and Long Rifle).
No. of Shots: 6.
Action: Single.
Barrel Length: 4 inches.
Overall Length: 8⅞ inches.
Weight: 17 ounces.
Sights: Fixed.
Finish: Blued; brass colored trigger guard.
Features: The one-piece frame is made of aluminum alloy. Cylinder is engraved steel; music wire springs are used.

Ruger—BLACKHAWK

Caliber: .357 Magnum.

No. of Shots: 6.

Action: Single.

Barrel Length: 4⅝, 6½, and 10-inch barrels are made.

Weight: Ranges from 39 ounces in the two shorter barrel lengths to 45 ounces with the 10-inch barrel.

Sights: Patridge style, ramp front blade, ⅛-inch wide and matted to minimize glare; adjustable rear sight (click screws).

Finish: Blued.

Grips: Walnut.

Features: This model is made on a heavy chrome-molybdenum steel frame. No leaf springs, music wire springs throughout. Note that the Blackhawk is also made in .44 Magnum, described separately.

Ruger—BLACKHAWK .44 MAGNUM

Barrel Length: 6½, 7½ and 10-inch barrels are made.
Weight: 40 ounces.
Features: Features are otherwise similar to the .357 Magnum
   Blackhawk.

Ruger—SUPER BLACKHAWK .44 MAGNUM

Barrel Length: 7½ inches only.
Overall Length: 13⅜ inches.
Trigger: ⅜ inch wide and serrated.
Features: Wide serrated hammer spur. The grip frame is specially
   strengthened and designed to minimize recoil of this heavy
   caliber. Straight back trigger guard.

Savage—MODEL 101

Caliber: .22 (Short, Long, and Long Rifle).
No. of Shots: Single Shot.
Action: Single action.
Barrel Length: 5½ inches.
Overall Length: 9 inches.
Weight: 20 ounces.
Sights: Fixed front; rear adjustable for windage.
Finish: Blued.
Grips: Wood.
Safety: Rebounding hammer.
Features: "Cylinder" is a part of the barrel which swings out to the
   right for push-rod ejection and loading. Frame is of aluminum
   alloy. Barrel and hammer are steel. The "cylinder" is non-
   functional and serves to lend this single shot the appearance
   of a Western six-shooter.

Sheridan—KNOCABOUT
(Model D)

Caliber: .22 (Short, Long, and Long Rifle).

No. of Shots: One.

Action: Single; barrel tips up from frame for unloading, ejection, and loading.

Barrel Length: 5 inches.

Weight: 24 ounces.

Sights: Fixed.

Finish: Blued.

Grips: Brown plastic.

Safety: Oversized rotary bolt, left side.

Features: Hammer spur is serrated; barrel catch release forward of trigger guard; positive extractor.

Smith and Wesson—.44 MAGNUM
(Model 29)

Caliber: .44 Magnum.

Ammunition: .44 Magnum, .44 S&W Special, and .44 S&W Russian.

No. of Shots: 6. (All S&W revolvers are six shot except certain models in .38 S&W.)

Action: Single and double; this is common to all S&W revolvers.

Barrel Length: 4, 6½, or 8⅜ inches.

Overall Length: With 6½-inch barrel, 11⅞ inches.

Weight: With 4-inch barrel, 43 ounces; 6½-inch barrel, 47 ounces; 8⅜-inch barrel, 51½ ounces.

Sights: Ramp front; micrometer click rear.

Finish: Blued or nickel.

Grips: Oversized and checkered.

Trigger: Grooved.

Features: Hammer, checked target type. Target grips of Goncalo Alves wood.

Smith and Wesson—.357 MAGNUM
(Model 27)

Caliber: Actual bullet diameter is .38 S&W Special.

Ammunition: .357 S&W Magnum, .38 S&W Special Hi-Speed, .38 S&W Special, and .38 S&W Special mid-range.

Barrel Length: 3½, 5, 6, 6½, and 8⅜ inches.

Overall Length: With 6-inch barrel, 11⅜ inches.

Weight: Varies from 41 ounces with short barrel to 47 ounces with longest barrel.

Sights: Several S&W front sights are available, some are target-adjustable; rear, fully adjustable micrometer click.

Finish: Blued or nickel.

Grips: Checkered walnut.

Features: Top strap and barrel rib finely checked.

Smith and Wesson—HIGHWAY PATROLMAN
(Model 28)

Caliber: .357 Magnum.
Ammunition: Same as for Model 27.
Barrel Length: 4 and 6 inches.
Overall Length: 11¼ inches with 6-inch barrel.
Weight: 41¾ ounces with shorter barrel.
Sights: Fixed front, quick-draw type; rear, adjustable micrometer
   click.
Finish: Blued. Stippling on barrel rib and frame edging.
Grips: Checkered walnut.

Smith and Wesson—1955 .45 TARGET
(Model 25)

Caliber: .45 ACP.

Ammunition: .45 ACP, .45 Auto-Rim, .45 Automatic Wad Cutter.

Barrel Length: 6½ inches.

Overall Length: 11⅞ inches.

Weight: 45 ounces.

Sights: Front, ⅛ inch plain Patridge-type; rear, adjustable micrometer click.

Finish: Blued.

Grips: Checkered walnut, target style.

Trigger: Grooved target type.

Features: Checked hammer spur, target type.

Smith and Wesson—.38/44 OUTDOORSMAN
(Model 23)

Caliber: .38 S&W.
Ammunition: Uses regular Special, Hi-Speed, and mid-range loads.
Barrel Length: 6½ inches.
Overall Length: 11¾ inches.
Weight: 41¾ ounces.
Sights: Plain Patridge front; adjustable micrometer click rear.
Finish: Blued.
Grips: Checkered walnut.

Smith and Wesson—1950 .44 TARGET
(Model 24)

Caliber: .44 S&W Special.
Ammunition: Also uses .44 S&W Russian.
Barrel Length: 6½ inches.
Overall Length: 11¾ inches.
Weight: 39½ ounces.
Sights: Fixed front; adjustable micrometer click rear.
Finish: Blued.
Grips: Checkered walnut.

Smith and Wesson—.38/44 HEAVY DUTY
(Model 20)

Ammunition: Uses both the S&W Special and Hi-Speed loads.
Barrel Length: 4, 5, and 6½ inches.
Overall Length: 10⅜ inches with 5-inch barrel.
Weight: 40 ounces with 5-inch barrel.
Sights: Fixed front; square-notch rear.
Finish: Blue or nickel.
Grips: Checkered walnut.

Smith and Wesson—1950 .44 MILITARY
(Model 21)

Ammunition: Uses both .44 S&W Special and .44 S&W Russian.
Barrel Length: 4, 5, and 6½ inches.
Overall Length: With 6½-inch barrel, 11¾ inches.
Weight: 39½ ounces with 6½-inch barrel.
Sights: Fixed.
Finish: Blued or nickel.
Grips: Checkered walnut.

Smith and Wesson—1950 ARMY
(Model 22)

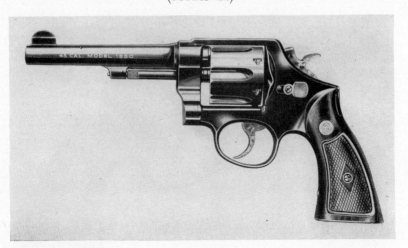

Caliber: .45 ACP.

Ammunition: Also uses .45 Auto-Rim and the Automatic Wad Cutter cartridges.

Barrel Length: 5½ inches.

Overall Length: 10¾ inches.

Weight: 36¼ ounces.

Sights: Fixed front and rear.

Finish: Blued.

Grips: Checkered walnut.

Smith and Wesson—.357 COMBAT MAGNUM
(Model 19)

Ammunition: Also uses .38 S&W Special (regular and Hi-Speed), and .38 S&W mid-range cartridges.

Barrel Length: 4 inches.

Overall Length: 9½ inches.

Weight: 35 ounces.

Sights: Quick-draw front; adjustable micrometer click rear.

Finish: Blued or nickel.

Grips: Checkered Goncalo Alves wood, target type.

Smith and Wesson—.38 MILITARY & POLICE
(Model 10)

Ammunition: .38 S&W Special and Special mid-range.
Barrel Length: 2, 4, 5, or 6 inches.
Overall Length: 9¼ inches with 4-inch barrel.
Weight: 30½ ounces with 4-inch barrel.
Sights: Fixed.
Finish: Blue or nickel.
Grips: Checkered walnut.

Smith and Wesson—.38 MILITARY & POLICE HEAVY BARREL
(Model 10)

Barrel Length: 4 inches.
Overall Length: 9¼ inches.
Weight: 34 ounces.
Sights: Fixed.
Finish: Blue or nickel.
Grips: Checkered walnut.
Features: This model is a heavier barreled version of the regular
Model 10, and uses the same ammunition.

Smith and Wesson—.38 MILITARY & POLICE AIRWEIGHT
(Model 12)

Ammunition: Uses the .38 S&W Special, regular and mid-range.
Barrel Length: 2 or 4 inches.
Overall Length: 6⅞ inches with 2-inch barrel, round butt.
Weight: 18 ounces with 2-inch barrel, round butt.
Sights: Fixed front and rear. Front ramp is serrated.
Finish: Blue or nickel.
Grips: Checkered walnut, round or square butt.
Features: Lightweight alloy frame, steel barrel and cylinder.

Smith and Wesson—MILITARY & POLICE (ROUND BUTT)
(Model 10)

Ammunition: .38 S&W Special, regular and mid-range.
Barrel Length: 2, 4, 5, and 6 inches.
Overall Length: With 2-inch barrel, 6⅞ inches.
Weight: 26 ounces with 2-inch barrel.
Sights: Fixed.
Finish: Blued or nickel.
Grips: Checkered walnut.

Smith and Wesson—.38 COMBAT MASTERPIECE
(Model 15)

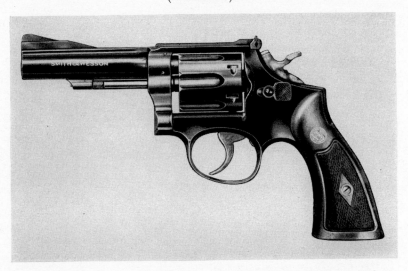

Ammunition: Uses both regular and mid-range loads.
Barrel Length: 4 inches.
Overall Length: 9⅛ inches.
Weight: 34 ounces (loaded).
Sights: Quick draw fixed front; adjustable micrometer click rear.
Finish: Blued.
Grips: Checkered walnut.

Smith and Wesson—K-22 MASTERPIECE
(Model 17)

Caliber: .22 (Short, Long, and Long Rifle).
Barrel Length: 6 or 8⅜ inches.
Overall Length: With 6-inch barrel, 11⅛ inches.
Weight: With 6-inch barrel, 38½ ounces; longer barrel, 42½ ounces.
Sights: Patridge front, adjustable micrometer click rear.
Finish: Blued.
Grips: Checkered walnut.

Smith and Wesson—K-22 MASTERPIECE M.R.F.
(Model 48)

Caliber: .22 Magnum Rimfire.
Barrel Length: 4, 6, 8⅜ inches.
Overall Length: With 6-inch barrel, 11⅛ inches.
Weight: With 6-inch barrel, 39 ounces.
Sights: Plain Patridge front; adjustable micrometer click rear.
Finish: Blued.
Grips: Checkered walnut.

Smith and Wesson—.22 MAGNUM
(Model 53)

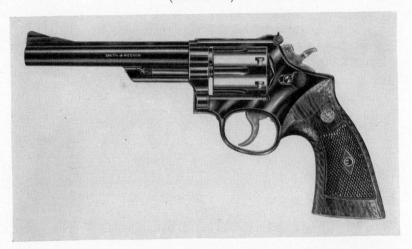

Ammunition: .22 Remington Jet Center-fire Magnum, or .22 Rimfire (Short, Long, and Long Rifle) when using inserts.

Barrel Length: 4, 6, 8⅜ inches.

Overall Length: With 6-inch barrel, 11¼ inches.

Weight: With 6-inch barrel, 40 ounces.

Sights: Quick draw front on plain ramp; adjustable micrometer
click rear.

Finish: Blued.

Grips: Checkered walnut, target style.

Features: .22 RF cartridges can be placed in inserts for cylinder
and used as alternatives to the standard .22 Remington Jet
cartridges.

Smith and Wesson—K-32 MASTERPIECE
(Model 16)

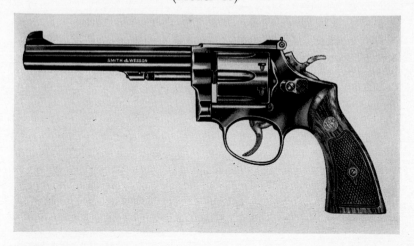

Caliber: .32 S&W Long.
Ammunition: Also uses wad-cutter and .32 S&W loads.
Barrel Length: 6 inches.
Overall Length: 11⅛ inches.
Weight: 38½ ounces.
Sights: Patridge fixed front; adjustable micrometer click rear.
Finish: Blued.
Grips: Checkered walnut.

Smith and Wesson—.22 COMBAT MASTERPIECE
(Model 18)

Ammunition: Uses .22 Short, Long, and Long Rifle.
Barrel Length: 4 inches.
Overall Length: 9⅛ inches.
Weight: 36½ ounces.
Sights: Quick draw fixed front; adjustable micrometer click rear.
Finish: Blued.
Grips: Checkered walnut.

Smith and Wesson—K-38 MASTERPIECE SINGLE ACTION
(Model 14)

Caliber: .38 S&W Special.

Ammunition: .38 S&W Special and .38 S&W Special mid-range.

Barrel Length: 6, 8⅜ inches.

Overall Length: With 6-inch barrel, 11⅛ inches.

Weight: With 6-inch barrel, 38½ ounces; 42½ ounces with longer barrel.

Sights: Front: Plain Patridge; adjustable micrometer click rear.

Finish: Blued.

Grips: Checkered walnut.

Hammer: Checked target type.

Trigger: Grooved target type.

Features: Special hammer, trigger, and hand-honed single action.

Smith and Wesson—K-38 MASTERPIECE
(Model 14)

Caliber: .38 S&W Special.
Barrel Length: 6, 8⅜ inches.
Overall Length: 11⅛ inches with 6-inch barrel.
Weight: 38½ ounces, short barrel; 42½ ounces, long barrel.
Sights: Fixed Patridge front; adjustable micrometer click rear.
Finish: Blued.
Grips: Checkered walnut.

Smith and Wesson—1953 .22/32 TARGET
(Model 35)

Caliber: .22 (Short, Long, and Long Rifle).
Barrel Length: 6 inches.
Overall Length: 10½ inches.
Weight: 25 ounces.
Sights: Patridge fixed front; adjustable micrometer click rear.
Finish: Blued.
Grips: Checkered walnut.

Smith and Wesson—1953 .22/32 KIT GUN
(Model 34)

Caliber: .22 (Short, Long, and Long Rifle).

Barrel Length: 2, 4 inches.

Overall Length: With 4-inch barrel, round butt, 8 inches.

Weight: 22½ ounces with 4-inch barrel, round butt.

Sights: Fixed ramp front, non-glare; adjustable micrometer click rear.

Finish: Blued or nickel.

Grips: Checkered walnut, either square or round butt.

Smith and Wesson—1955 .22/32 KIT GUN AIRWEIGHT
(Model 43)

Barrel Length: 3½ inches.
Overall Length: 8 inches.
Weight: 14¼ ounces.
Features: Lightweight alloy frame, steel barrel and cylinder. All other specifications similar to Model 34 except as cited.

Smith and Wesson—1960 .22/32 KIT GUN M.R.F.
(Model 51)

Caliber: .22 Magnum Rimfire.
Barrel Length: 3½ inches.
Overall Length: 8 inches.
Weight: 24 ounces.
Sights: Serrated ramp front; adjustable micrometer click rear.
Finish: Blued or nickel.
Grips: Checkered walnut, either square or round butt.

Smith and Wesson—.32 HAND EJECTOR
(Model 30)

Ammunition: .32 S&W, .32 S&W Long, .32 S&W Long wad cutter.
Barrel Length: 2, 3, or 4 inches.
Overall Length: With 4-inch barrel, 8 inches.
Weight: With 4-inch barrel, 18 ounces.
Sights: Serrated ramp front, square-notch rear; both sights are fixed.
Finish: Blued or nickel.
Grips: Checkered walnut; round butt.

Smith and Wesson—.32 REGULATION POLICE
(Model 31)

Ammunition: Uses .32 S&W, .32 S&W Long, and .32 S&W Long
    wad cutter.
Barrel Length: 2, 3, or 4 inches.
Overall Length: With 4-inch barrel, 8½ inches.
Weight: With 4-inch barrel, 18¾ ounces.
Sights: Ramp front, square-notch rear, both fixed.
Finish: Blued or nickel.
Grips: Checkered walnut.

Smith and Wesson—.38 TERRIER
(Model 32)

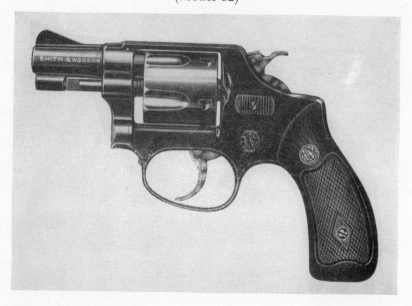

Ammunition: .38 S&W.
No. of Shots: 5.
Barrel Length: 2 inches.
Overall Length: 6¼ inches.
Weight: 17 ounces.
Sights: Ramp front, square-notch rear, both fixed.
Finish: Blued or nickel.
Grips: Checkered walnut, round butt.

Smith and Wesson—.38 REGULATION POLICE
(Model 33)

Ammunition: .38 S&W
No. of Shots: 5.
Barrel Length: 4 inches.
Overall Length: 8½ inches.
Weight: 18 ounces.
Sights: Fixed; ramp front, square notch rear.
Finish: Blued or nickel.
Grips: Checkered walnut, square butt.

Smith and Wesson—.38 CHIEFS SPECIAL
(Model 36)

Ammunition: .38 S&W Special and Special mid-range.

No. of Shots: 5.

Barrel Length: 2 or 3 inches.

Overall Length: 6½ inches with short barrel, round butt.

Weight: 19 ounces with short barrel and round butt.

Sights: Fixed. Front is shallow ramp, rear is square notched.

Finish: Blued or nickel.

Grips: Checkered walnut, round or square butt.

Smith and Wesson—.38 CHIEFS SPECIAL AIRWEIGHT
(Model 37)

Ammunition: Same as Model 36.

No. of Shots: 5.

Weight: With 2-inch barrel and round butt, 14 ounces.

Features: Except for weight, specifications are comparable to the Model 36. Lightweight alloy frame, steel barrel and cylinder.

Smith and Wesson—BODYGUARD AIRWEIGHT
(Model 38)

Ammunition: .38 S&W Special and Special mid-range.
No. of Shots: 5.
Barrel Length: 2 inches.
Overall Length: 6⅜ inches.
Weight: 14½ ounces—alloy frame, steel barrel and cylinder.
Sights: Fixed front and rear. Front is serrated ramp, well smoothed.
Finish: Blued or nickel.
Grips: Checkered walnut, round butt.
Features: This model is constructed with high receiver walls brought back and rounded off to prevent the hammer from catching on the lining of a pocket. The hammer, while shrouded, has a serrated spur extending for hand cocking.

    Note: A 20½-ounce version in all-steel construction is known as the Model 49. Like the Model 38 it is finished in either blue or nickel.

Smith and Wesson—CENTENNIAL
(Model 40)

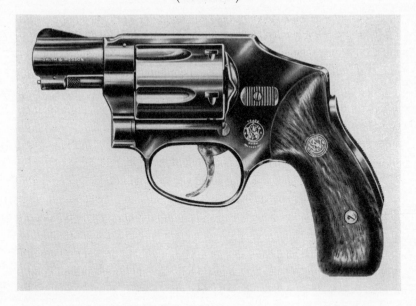

Ammunition: .38 S&W Special and .38 S&W Special mid-range.

No. of Shots: 5.

Barrel Length: 2 inches.

Overall Length: 6½ inches.

Weight: 19 ounces, all-steel construction.

Sights: Fixed front and rear, both smoothed and will not catch on clothing.

Finish: Blued or nickel.

Grips: Smooth walnut with rounded butt.

Safety: A grip safety protrudes from the rear of the grip unless the revolver is held firmly.

Features: Though the receiver walls are brought back high to conceal the hammer, they are lightly concaved and thus distinguished from the receiver of the Model 38 and Model 49. The Centennial is a pocket gun which will not catch on clothing when carried.

Note: It is also made in Airweight construction; the lightweight version is known as the Model 42 and weighs only 13 ounces. Model 42 is available in blue or nickel.

Smith and Wesson—.38 MASTER
(Model 52)

Ammunition: .38 S&W Special mid-range wad cutter only.

No. of Shots: Magazine holds 5 rounds.

Action: Semi-automatic.

Barrel Length: 5 inches.

Overall Length: 8⅝ inches.

Weight: 41 ounces with empty magazine.

Sights: Patridge front, micrometer click rear (fully adjustable). The sighting radius measures 6¹⁵⁄₁₆ inches.

Finish: Blued. Sighting area is sandblast finish against glare.

Grips: Checkered walnut.

Trigger: ⅜ inch width, grooved, and has adjustable trigger stop.

Smith and Wesson—.22 AUTOMATIC PISTOL
(Model 41)

Caliber: Either .22 Long Rifle or .22 Short.

No. of Shots: Magazine holds 10 rounds.

Barrel Length: 7⅜ inches. Barrel is grooved for Olympic counter-weights.

Overall Length: 12 inches (with muzzle brake attached).

Weight: 43½ ounces.

Sights: ⅛-inch Patridge, undercut; fully adjustable micrometer click rear. Sighting radius is 9⁵⁄₁₆ inches.

Finish: Blued.

Grips: Checkered walnut, modified thumb rest. Stocks are designed to be adaptable to either right or left-handed shooters.

Trigger: ⅜ inch width, grooved, with adjustable trigger stop.

Features: Detachable muzzle brake. The .22 Short version is designed for international competitive shooting.

Smith and Wesson—.22 AUTOMATIC PISTOL
(Model 41)

Ammunition: .22 Long Rifle.
Barrel Length: 5 inches.
Overall Length: 8⅜ inches.
Weight: 37½ ounces.
Sights: Sighting radius is 7⅜ inches, otherwise virtually the same as model opposite.
Features: This is the shorter barreled version of the Model 41.

Smith and Wesson—.22 AUTOMATIC PISTOL
(Model 46)

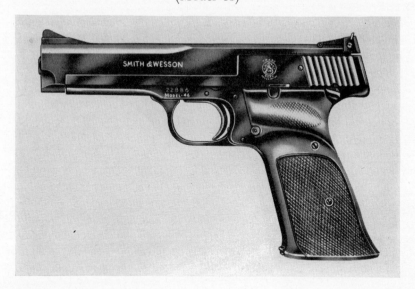

Caliber: .22 Long Rifle.

No. of Shots: 10 rounds in magazine.

Barrel Length: 5 inches.

Overall Length: 8%6 inches.

Weight: 38¼ ounces.

Sights: Serrated ramp front, fully adjustable micrometer click rear.
Sighting radius is 7⅚6 inches.

Finish: Blued.

Grips: Molded Nylon with modified thumb rest.

Trigger: Wide, grooved with adjustable trigger stop.

Smith and Wesson—.22 AUTOMATIC PISTOL
(Model 46)

Barrel Length: 7 inches; grooved for Olympic counterweights.
Overall Length: 10⁹⁄₁₆ inches.
Weight: 42 ounces.
Sights: Patridge undercut front, adjustable micrometer click rear.
  Sighting radius is 9⁵⁄₁₆ inches.
Finish: Blued.
Grips: Molded Nylon with modified thumb rest.
Features: This is the longer barreled version of the Model 46.

Smith and Wesson—9mm AUTOMATIC PISTOL
(DOUBLE ACTION)
(Model 39)

Ammunition: 9mm Luger and Parabellum.

No of Shots: Magazine holds 8 rounds.

Barrel Length: 4 inches.

Overall Length: $7\frac{7}{16}$ inches.

Weight: $26\frac{1}{2}$ ounces (without magazine).

Sights: Serrated ramp front. Rear is micrometer click adjustable for windage only.

Finished: Blued or nickel.

Grips: Checkered walnut.

CHAPTER 9

Collector's Guide
To Values

A basic principle of economics is that a purchase is made when the buyer's subjective evaluation of an item equals, or exceeds, the seller's objective value placed on an item.

If an individual's financial resources are not limited, he will frequently pay whatever is asked for an item which he desires ardently at the earliest possible time. However, the great majority of persons interested in pursuing gun collecting as a hobby are of limited resources. Thus they are obliged, if they are cautious, to consider this hobby from the viewpoint of a sound economic investment.

Handguns, or any firearms, in excellent condition represent the safest and soundest investment with respect to potential, or forced, resale. For this reason the author considers it most practical for the majority of readers of this book to attach only one value to every handgun listed— that value representing the top dollar a collector is advised to invest in that particular handgun when found in "Excellent" condition (as defined by the National Rifle Association). These values are such that the buyer may retain reasonable confidence that he will not take a loss in the event he is obliged to unload an item within a short period of time following purchase. No one can foresee an impending economic depression with resultant falling market for hobby items. The assumption is here made that collectors' items of the nature described in this book

217

will continue to become scarcer as time goes by and consequently will continue to increase in dollar value—even faster if the U.S. economy continues at a slightly inflationary pace.

The values cited are not "off the top of the author's head"—a situation which is suspected to be the case with some other similar listings in print. The author has (by actual count) attended 56 "gun shows" sponsored by gun collectors associations within the four-year period, 1958-1961. He is a Director, as well as Historian, of the world's largest gun collectors association—the Ohio Gun Collectors Association, Inc. whose Columbus meetings routinely exceed 500 tables of exhibits. He has personally observed and studied closely the price range of most makes and models of cartridge handguns and in addition has at his disposal composite records of actual sales of many of the items listed which were transacted at collectors meetings around the country within the recent past.

Again, the prices cited are for standard production models. If a handgun, in addition to being generally excellent, is engraved, was once owned by a famous person, has "custom" finish or grips, or is in unfired "as new" condition, it is worth somewhat more than the figure given here. How much more is dependent upon too many possible aspects to be put in monetary, or percentage, terms as it is a relative matter and must be left to the discretion and discrimination of the buyer. Neither can the potential buyer be advised specifically how much less to pay for a specimen below the condition of "Excellent." This again depends upon multiple factors such as availability of the particular model in any condition, how long the buyer is willing to wait to acquire an excellent specimen, the need for the particular model to further completion of a "type" collection, etc.

The National Rifle Association has adopted two sets of condition standards for describing firearms; one applicable to "antique" firearms and the other applicable to "modern" firearms.

"Antique" is a rather vague term but, as defined by Webster's dictionary, implies "old-fashioned, of a bygone style or time." The term "modern" implies "current, or recent past."

With respect to the era of cartridge handguns, we can consider handguns produced during the period 1857-1910 as logically falling under the "antique" category and those produced during the period 1910-1962 as falling under the "modern" category as regards condition standards. This is admittedly arbitrary but on the whole convenient and defensible.

The N.R.A. definition of "Excellent" as applied to "antique" firearms is as follows: "All original parts; over 80% original finish; sharp lettering, numerals and design on metal and wood; unmarred wood; fine bore."

The N.R.A. definition of "Excellent" as applied to "modern" firearms is as follows: "New condition, used but little, no noticeable marring of wood or metal, finish perfect (except at muzzle or sharp edges)."

No handgun models in current production have been listed. The buying policy adopted by the author with respect to current models is as follows: For factory-new, unfired guns—wholesale, or approximately 75% of retail list price; for used guns in excellent to perfect condition— not over 60% of retail list price. This policy is not necessarily advocated for the reader but the author considers it to be basically sound from an investment standpoint.

COLLECTOR'S GUIDE TO VALUES
REVOLVERS

MAKE and MODEL   VALUE

Colt

Patent House Pistol, "cloverleaf" cyl., .41 RF	$135
Same, with round cyl.	115
Open Top (Old Line) Pocket, .22 RF	50
Same, with ejector housing	175
Single Action Army, 1873, .45 Colt	110
Frontier Six-Shooter, .44-40	150
Storekeeper's without ejector	160
Bisley	120
Bisley Target, flat top-strap	200
New Line Pocket, .22	50
Same, .32	45
Same, .38	45
Same, .41	50
New Police (Police & Thug), .38	175
New House, .38, .41	95
Double Action, "Lightning", .38	75
Double Action, "Thunderer", .41	75
Double Action Army, or Frontier, .45	85
New Double Action Army & Navy, .38	75
Alaskan Double Action, .44-40	95
New Service	55
New Service Target, .44, .45	90
Marine Corps, 1905 D.A., .38	85
1917 Army, D. A., .45	32
Shooting Master Target, .38, .357, .44, .45	120
Pocket Positive, .32	55
New Police, .32	50
Police Positive, .22, .32, .38	40
Police Positive Target, .22	60
Police Positive Special, .32-20	75
Officers Model Target, .38, .22	65
Officers Model Special, .38, .22	65
Army Special, .38	55
Same, .32-20	75
Banker's Special, .38	65
Same, .22	120

MAKE and MODEL   VALUE

Harrington & Richardson

Wesson & Harrington, 1871, .22	$ 45
Same, .32	35
Same, .38	35
Wesson & Harrington (no ejector)	25
Automatic Ejecting	20
Same, with folding knife	85
Premier	20
Hammerless, light frame	20
Hammerless, heavy frame	18
American	16
Young America	16
Vest Pocket	22
Model 4, Model 5, .32, .38	16
Model 6, .22	20
Sportsman, Model 199 S.A., .22	45
Ultra Sportsman, .22	65
Eureka Sportsman, .22	65
New Defender, .22	35
Model 699 (thumb ejector), .22	30
Target, .22	25
22 Special, .22	28
Expert, .22	28
Trapper, .22	32
Hunter, .22	40
Defender, .38	28

High Standard

All High Standard revolvers are current and thus no
values are cited.

Hopkins & Allen

Blue Jacket No. 1, or No. 1½, .22	18
Blue Jacket No. 2, .32	15
Czar, .22	16
Dictator, .32	14
XL No. 1, .22	18
XL No. 2, .30	12
XL No. 3, .32	15
XL No. 4, .38	15
XL No. 5, .38	22

MAKE and MODEL　　　　　　　　　　　　　VALUE

Hopkins & Allen (Continued)

XL No. 6, or No. 7, .41	$ 18
Ranger No. 1, .22	18
Ranger No. 2, .32	15
XL Navy, .38	85
Army, 1876, .44-40	85
XL Series, double action	18
Hammer "Automatic," .32, .38	18
Hammerless "Automatic," .32, .38	16
Forehand Model, .32, .38	22
Safety Police (triple action), .22	35
Same, .32	30
Same, .38	30

Iver Johnson

Single Action Models: Favorite, Tycoon, Encore, Favorite Navy, Smoker, Defender, Defender 89; .22	18
Other calibers	15
Eagle (1st double action)	22
American Bulldog	16
1879 Double Action (Swing out cyl.)	35
Boston Bulldog	14
Swift, D.A.	26
Safety "Automatic," hammer	22
Safety "Automatic," hammerless	20
Model 1900, D.A.	15
Model 1900 Target, .22	18
U. S. Revolver Co. (hammer), .32, .38	16
Same (hammerless), .32, .38	14
I. J. Petite (baby hammerless), .22	40
Supershot Sealed Eight, Mod. 833, .22	25
Target Sealed Eight, .22	18
Trigger Cocking Target, .22	55
Supershot, Mod. 844 (D.A.), .22	30
Armsworth, Mod. 855 (S.A.), .22	30

Remington

Zig-Zag, (ring trigger, D.A.), .22	300
New Line No. 1 (Smoot), .30	35
New Line No. 2 (Smoot), .32	45

MAKE and MODEL   VALUE

Remington (Continued)

New Line No. 3 (Smoot), .38 .... $ 45

New Line No. 4 (Smoot), .38, .41   55

1875 Army (metal web under bbl.), .44-40   200

1890 Army (no web under bbl.), .44-40   300

Iroquois, .22   75

Mexican (D.A. top-break), .38   60

Ruger

Single-Six (lightweight frame), .22   50

All other Ruger revolvers current.

Smith & Wesson

Model No. 1—1st Issue, .22   300

Model No. 1—2nd Issue, .22   55

Model No. 1—3rd Issue, .22   45

Model No. 2, .32   45

Model No. 2 ("Army" 6" bbl.), .32   65

Model No. 1½—1st Issue, .32   45

Model No. 1½—2nd Issue, .32   40

New Model No. 1½ (New Model 32), .32   35

New Model No. 2 ("Baby Russian"), .38   60

Model No. 3 American, .44   150

Model No. 3 Russian (so marked), .44   200

Model No. 3 Schofield, .45   140

New Model No. 3 American, .44   175

Model 32 Double Action—1st Issue, .32   45

Model 32 D.A.—2nd & 3rd Issues, .32   35

Model 32 Safety Hammerless (any), .32   40

Model 38 Safety Hammerless—1st Issue, .38   75

Model 38 Safety Hammerless—2nd Issue, .38   60

Model 38 Safety Hammerless—3rd, 4th, 5th Issue, .38 ..   50

Model 38 Double Action (any issue), .38   45

Model 38 Perfected D.A., .38   80

Model "I" Hand Ejector—1st Issue, .32   85

Regulation Police, .32   35

Regulation Police, .38   40

Military & Police (old style rd. butt), .38   65

Model 44 Double Action, .44   65

Model 44 D.A. Frontier, .44   75

MAKE and MODEL   VALUE

Smith & Wesson (Continued)

New Century—"Triple Lock," .44 .... $110
Model 32-20 Hand Ejector, .32 65
Model of 1891 Single Action, .38 90
Model "M" Hand Ejector—"Ladysmith," .22
    1st Issue 160
    2nd Issue 140
    3rd Issue 135
    6″ bbl.—3rd Issue 225
Model 22/32 Hand Ejector—"Bekeart," .22 65
Model 1917 Army, .45 35
Victory Model (WW. II), .38 28

MISCELLANEOUS

MAKE and MODEL   VALUE

Aetna Arms .... $ 15
Allen, Ethan (side-hammer) 35
Allen & Wheelock (side-hammer) 35
American Arms—Ring Extractor, S.A. 35
American Standard Tool, .22 30
Bacon (name brands) 15
"Navy," .38 125
Bliss & Goodyear (name brands) 15
Brooklyn Arms (front-loading) 50
Cody "Thunderbird," .22 18
Cone, D.D. (with ejector) 45
Connecticut Arms (front-loading) 40
Deringer Rifle & Pistol Works, .22 60
Same, .32 50
Dickinson, E. L. 35
Eagle Firearms (front-loading) 40

Forehand & Wadsworth
Russian Model 32 16
Side-hammer models 30
"Terror," .32 18
"British Bulldog," .38 20
"Swamp Angel," .41 28
Old Model Army, .44 95
New Model Army, .44 85

MAKE and MODEL   VALUE

Fryberg, Andrew .... $ 20
Grant, W. L. (with ejector) 45
Hood Fire Arms (name brands) 15
Kolb "Baby Hammerless," .32 & .22 25
Lee Arms "Red Jacket" series 18
Lowell Arms, .22 25
Lower, J. P. (with ejector) 45
Maltby, Henley (tang-safety, hammerless) 22
Manhattan, .22 45
    Same, .32 35
Marlin
    "Little Joker," .22 60
    "OK," .22 50
    "Standard" (any) 32
    Double Action, T.B. 45
Merwin, Hulbert—Pocket Army, .44 60
    Pocket Models, .32, .38 40
Moore (front-loading) 40
    Rear-loading 55
National Arms (front-loading) 40
Osgood "Duplex," .32 & .22 85
Plant "Army" cup-primer, .42 60
    Rear loading, .22 25
Pond, L. W. "Army," .44 95
    Separate chambers 55
    Rear-loading 45
Prescott, E. A. "Navy," .38 85
    Spur trigger models 55
Reid, James "Reid's Ex'tr," .41 150
    Knuckleduster, with bbl., .32 165
Rollin White "Made for Smith & Wesson," .22 60
    Same, .32 50
Rome Revolver & Novelty 18
Rupertus "Empire," .22 36
    "Empire," .38 32
    "Empire 41," .41 40
Ryan, T. E. "Ryan's New Model," .32 18
    "Napoleon," .22 20
    "Napoleon," .32 18

MAKE and MODEL   VALUE

Ryan, T. E. (Continued)

"Marquis of Lorne," .32 .... $ 16

Sedgley, R. F. "Baby Hammerless," .22 25

Shattuck Arms (swing-out cyl.), .32, .38 35

Smith, Otis A. Smith's Patent April 15, 1873 28

Model 1883 Shell Ejector 35

Standard Revolver (any) 32

Union (semi-automatic), .32 90

U. S. Revolver (see Iver Johnson)

Warner, James .30 40

Wesson & Harrington (see Harrington & Richardson)

Whitney Arms (Whitneyville Armory), .22 36

Same, .32 28

Same, .38 32

Wright Arms "Little All Right," .22 125

SINGLE SHOT PISTOLS

MAKE and MODEL   VALUE

Allen, Ethan—1865 Derringer, .32 .... $ 45

Same, .41 55

Allen & Wheelock .22 30

Same, .41 45

Bacon .32 30

Ballard—Derringer, .41 70

Brown "Southerner" Derringer, .41 55

Colt

No. 1 Deringer, .41 200

No. 2 Deringer, .41 110

No. 3 Deringer, .41 85

Camp Perry, .22 120

Connecticut Arms & Mnfg. "Hammond Bulldog," .44 65

Continental Arms .22 22

Cowles .22 28

Dickinson (rack-and-pinion extractor), .22 75

Dickinson .32 65

Forehand & Wadsworth—Derringer, .41 80

MAKE and MODEL   VALUE

Harrington & Richardson
  "Model U.S.R.A." .22 .... $ 95
  "Handygun," .22 65
  Same, .32-20 75
  Same, .410 65
  Same, 28 ga. 55
Hartford .22 50
Hopkins & Allen
  "Ladies Garter Pistol," .22 125
  "New Model Target," .22 30
  XL Derringer, .41 65
Iver Johnson "Star Vest Pocket" Derr., .22 40
  "Eclipse" Derr., .32 35
Lombard .22 30
  .32 25
Marlin
  "Vest Pocket," .22 30
  "OK," .22 25
  "Never Miss," .22 40
  Same, .32 35
  Same, .41 55
  "Victor," .38 45
Merrimac "Southerner" Derringer, .41 60
Moore—1863 all-metal Derringer, .41 85
National—No. 1 all-metal Derringer, .41 125
  No. 2 Derringer, .41 85
Remington
  "Vest Pocket," .22 60
  "Vest Pocket" (split breech-block), .41 85
  Remington-Elliot Derringer, .41 95
  1866 Navy, .50 300
  1867 Navy, .50 125
  1871 Army, .50 125
  1891 Target, .44, .22 125
  1901 Target, .44, .22 135
Rollin White, 1858, .32, .38 60
Rupertus .22 45
  Other cals. 35

MAKE and MODEL   VALUE

Sydney Manson "S-M Sporter," .22	$ 18
Smith & Wesson	
"Model of 1891"—1st Issue, .22	110
Same, .32	95
Same, .38	95
"Model of 1891"—2nd Issue, .22	120
"Perfected," .22	100
"Straight Line," .22	125
"Straight Line" (cased), .22	175
Stafford .22	40
Starr—Button trigger Derringer, .41	110
Stevens	
"Kick Up," .22	65
"Gem," .22	35
"Gould," .22	95
"Conlin," .22	80
"Lord," .22	90
"Diamond," .22	35
"Off-Hand Target" Model 35, .22	45
"Model 10 Target," .22	40
"Autoshot" Model 35, .410	60
"Tip Up," Model 41, .22	35
Terry, J. C.—Derringer, .22	65
Varsity—Tompkins Target, .22	120
Wamo "Powermaster," .22	25
Wesson, F., .22	35
Wurfflein, W., 1884, .22	70

MULTIPLE SHOT PISTOLS

MAKE and MODEL   VALUE

American Arms (Wheeler's Patents), .41-.41	$ 85
Caliber .32-.32	65
Caliber .22-.32	65
Bacon-Pepperbox, .22	80
Chicago "Protector," .32	85
Continental "Ladies Companion," .22	110
Fiala—Magazine Pistol, .22	45
Marble Arms "Game Getter," .22-.410	85

MAKE and MODEL VALUE

Marston—3 bbl. Knife Pistol, .22 .... $175
   3 bbl. (Without knife), .32 85
   3 bbl. "Improved 1864," .32 95
Minneapolis "Protector," .32 80
Mossberg "Novelty" pepperbox, .22 80
   "Brownie" pepperbox, .22 40
Osgood "Duplex," .32-.22 85
Reid, James "My Friend" knuckleduster, .22 75
   Same, .32 65
   Same, .41 150
Remington—Rem.-Elliot pepperbox, .22 85
   Same, .32 75
   Double Derringer, O/U, .41 60
   "Rem.-Rider" magazine pistol, .32 120
Rupertus—2 bbl. (side X side), .22 75
   1864 pepperbox, .22 110
Sharps—4 bbl. 1859 pepperbox, .22 65
   Same, .32 65
Shattuck "Unique" pepperbox, .22 80
   Same, .32 75
Starr—4 bbl. button-trigger, .32 85
   Same, .41 100
Wesson, F.
   "Vest Pocket" O/U, .22 125
   Superposed, .22 90
   Same, .41 90
   Superposed (with knife), .32 120
   Same, .41 130

SEMI-AUTOMATIC PISTOLS

MAKE and MODEL VALUE

Colt
   1900 Sporting, .38 .... $ 90
   1902 Sporting, .38 80
   1902 Military, .38 100
   1903 Pocket, .38 60
   1903 Pocket, .32 45
   1908 Pocket, .380 45
   1905 Military, .45 125

MAKE and MODEL   VALUE

Colt (Continued)
   1911 Military, .45 .... $ 45
   1911-A1, .45 45
   1908 Pocket, .25 50
   Target (pre-Woodsman), .22 80
   Woodsman—1st Issue, .22 70
   Match Target Woodsman—1st Issue, .22 90
   Ace Target, .22 90
   Ace Service, .22 110
   National Match, 1st Issue, .45 100

Grant Hammond—1915 Gov't., .45 250

Harrington & Richardson—Self-Loading, .25 45
   Self-Loading, .32 35

Hartford .22 55

High Standard
   B (.22) 45
   C (.22 Short only) 35
   S-B (.22 Shot only) 100
   A (.22) 35
   D (.22) 45
   E (.22) 60
   H-D Military (.22) 40
   G—.380 45
   G-B (.22) 35
   G-D (.22) 45
   G-E (.22) 60
   Olympic—1st Issue (.22 Short) 60
   Olympic—2nd Issue (.22 Short) 60
   Supermatic—1st Issue (.22) 55
   Field King (.22) 40
   Flite King—lightweight (.22) 35

Kimball (Fires .30 U.S. carbine) 100

Phoenix—.25 110

Reising—.22 60

Remington—Model 51, .32 40
   Model 51, .380 45

Ruger (All models current.)

MAKE and MODEL   VALUE

Savage
  1907, .32 .... $ 30
  Same, .380 32
  1915 (Hammerless), .32 36
  Same, .380 40
  1917, .32 36
  Same, .380 40
  1905 Military, .45 200
  Pocket, .25 125
Smith & Wesson Pocket hammerless, .35 70
  Pocket hammerless, .32 175
  Model 44 Single Action, 9mm 95
Union (A semi-automatic revolver), .32 90
Warner (Davis-Warner) "Infallible," .32 40
Whitney "Wolverine," .22 30

BIBLIOGRAPHY
OF
SUGGESTED READINGS

The suggested readings here listed will provide more detailed information with respect to some makes and models of American cartridge handguns. The careful reader will occasionally note discrepancies between alleged factual material cited in these readings and those cited by the author. The author has made every endeavor to ascertain the validity of factual data and to avoid the perpetuation of errors. How well he has succeeded will be determined by the test of time.

BOOKS
Carey, A. Merwyn, *American Firearms Makers,* Thomas Y. Crowell Company, New York, N. Y., 1953

Jacobs, C. R., *Official Gun Book,* Crown Publishers, Inc., New York, N.Y., 1950.

Karr, C. L. & C. R., *Remington Handguns,* The Stackpole Company, Harrisburg, Pa., 1947

Leyson, Burr, *The High Standard Pistol Guide,* Greenberg, New York, N. Y., 1954

McHenry, R. C. & Roper W. F., *Smith & Wesson Handguns,* The Stackpole Company, Harrisburg, Pa., 1958

Parsons, John E., *Smith & Wesson Revolvers,* William Morrow & Company, Inc., New York, N.Y., 1957

Serven, James E., *Colt Firearms—1836-1954,* Serven, Santa Ana, Calif., 1954

Smith, Walter H. B., *The Book of Pistols & Revolvers,* The Stackpole Company, Harrisburg, Pa., 1960

Stoeger, *The Shooter's Bible—No. 33,* Stoeger Arms Corp., Long Island City, N.Y., 1941

Ulrich, A. L., *A Century of Achievement,* Colt's Patent Fire Arms Manufacturing Co., Inc., Hartford, Conn., 1937

Webster, Donald B., Jr., *Suicide Specials,* The Stackpole Company, Harrisburg, Pa., 1958

Winant, Lewis, *Firearms Curiosa,* St. Martin's Press, Inc., New York, N.Y., 1961

ARTICLES
Askins, Col. Charles, "S&W's Modern 9 m/m Automatic," *Guns & Ammo,* June, 1961

Berg, Paul O., "The Hopkins & Allen Guns" *The Gun Report,* December, 1961

Logan, Herschel C., "J. M. Marlin's Handguns" *The American Rifleman,* October, 1958

"All Metal Pistols" *The American Rifleman,* November, 1958

233

Logan (Continued)
"The Front-Loading Plant" *The American Rifleman*, April, 1959
"Cartridge Pepperboxes" *The American Rifleman*, October, 1959
"E. A. Prescott and His Revolvers" *The American Rifleman*, September, 1960
"The L. W. Pond Revolvers" *The American Rifleman*, January, 1961
"The 4-Shot Mossberg Pistols" *The American Rifleman*, March 1961
McConnell, Duncan, "Who Made The Infallible Pistol?" *The Gun Report*, August, 1960
Moreton, David O., "New Olympic Free Pistol" *Guns & Ammo*, July, 1960
Peterson, Harold L., "Firearms Museums—U.S. & Canada" *The American Rifleman*, January, 1960
Sell, DeWitt E., "The Vanishing American Single Shot" *Guns & Ammo*, May, 1960
"Iver Johnson Firearms" *The American Rifleman*, May, 1961
"The Sixgun Grows Up" *Guns & Ammo*, August, 1961
"Harrington & Richardson Handguns," *The American Rifleman*, July, 1962
Simmons, Donald, "Remington Automatic Pistol" *Guns*, November, 1958
"Remington's Double Deringer" *Guns & Ammo*, August, 1959
"Smith & Wesson's .35 Auto" *Guns & Ammo*, August, 1960
Stern, Daniel K., "Savage Pocket Pistols," *The American Rifleman*, September, 1962
Triggs, James M., "Ruger 'Blackhawk' .357 Revolver" *The American Rifleman*, March, 1957
"Colt Single Action Army Revolver" *The American Rifleman*, August, 1958
"Smith & Wesson Model 39" *The American Rifleman*, December, 1958
"Smith & Wesson Number 1 Revolver" *The American Rifleman*, March, 1959
"Colt Double Action Revolver" *The American Rifleman*, June, 1959
"Smith & Wesson Military & Police Revolver" *The American Rifleman*, January, 1961
"Colt Deringer No. 3" *The American Rifleman*, February, 1961
"Smith & Wesson Model 41-46 Pistol" *The American Rifleman*, August, 1961
"S & W New Departure Safety Hammerless Revolver" *The American Rifleman*, December, 1961
Wessel, Thomas E., "Hi-Standard Supermatic Trophy Pistol" *The American Rifleman*, May, 1960
"Ruger Single-Six Revolver" *The American Rifleman*, July, 1960
"Hi-Standard Sentinel Revolver" *The American Rifleman*, November, 1960

INDEX

235